LANGUAGE EXPERIENCE AND
EARLY LANGUAGE DEVELOPMENT

Language Experience and Early Language Development: From Input to Uptake

Margaret Harris
Royal Holloway and Bedford New College,
University of London, U.K.

LEA LAWRENCE ERLBAUM ASSOCIATES, PUBLISHERS LEA
Hove (UK)   Hillsdale (USA)

Copyright © 1992 by Lawrence Erlbaum Associates Ltd.
  All rights reserved. No part of this book may be reproduced in any
  form, by photostat, microform, retrieval system, or any other
  means without the prior written permission of the publisher.

Lawrence Erlbaum Associates Ltd., Publishers
27 Palmeira Mansions
Church Road
Hove
East Sussex, BN3 2FA
U.K.

British Library Cataloguing in Publication Data

Harris, Margaret
  Language Experience and Early Language Development: From
  Input to Uptake. —
  (Essays in Developmental Psychology Series, ISSN 0959-3977)
  I. Title   II. Series
  401

  ISBN 0-86377-231-5 (Hbk)
  ISBN 0-86377-238-2 (Pbk)
  ISSN 0959-3977

Printed and bound in the United Kingdom by BPCC Wheatons Limited, Exeter

For Catherine and Matthew

Contents

Preface

When I first began research into children's language development I was an ardent nativist. In many ways I remain so, even though my interest in environmental influences on language development might be seen as running completely counter to nativist views. To my mind, it is perfectly consistent to believe that, while much of language development is governed by the operation of powerful innate principles, some important aspects of early language development are significantly influenced by the child's language experience.

This issue is not only of theoretical interest. Understanding how the child's language development is related to experience has important implications for children whose early language development is giving cause for concern. If there are no environmental influences on early development, then little can be done to help the child whose first steps into language are faltering. But, if the speed with which children develop language is subject to some external influence, then there are likely to be opportunities for successful intervention. I hope to show that there are grounds for optimism rather than pessimism in this area.

The book falls into three parts. In the first four chapters, I discuss the general background to the issues that I am considering. In the next four, I describe a series of longitudinal studies that I have carried out into linguistic input to children and its relationship to early language development. The final chapter attempts to draw some practical and theoretical conclusions.

The first chapter in the book provides an overview of some of the theoretical controversy relating to fundamental questions about the nature of language development. The second chapter presents a review of research into parental speech to young children and considers whether there is any evidence for a causal link between parental speech and child language development. In Chapter 3, I consider the wider social context of the child's language experience and discuss the work of Halliday and Bruner and, in the fourth chapter, I discuss the methodological problems inherent in investigations of the relationship between language development and language experience .

The next four chapters draw on my own research. In Chapter 5, I examine the relationship between young children's socio-linguistic experience and their early language development. In Chapter 6, I discuss early vocabulary development and its relationship to maternal language and, in Chapter 7, I describe a detailed study of the relationship between early vocabulary development and maternal speech. Chapter 8 is devoted to a consideration of potential problems with language development that are encountered by deaf children and I consider how deaf children acquire their first signs.

Chapter 9 begins with a discussion of the early language development of blind children in relation to other issues discussed in the book. I end by drawing out some of the theoretical implications of the research findings and attempting the Herculean task of relating issues about environmental influences on early language development to recent ideas about innate constraints.

Margaret Harris
London, January 1992

Acknowledgements

The studies that I describe in this book could not have been carried out without the invaluable assistance of a dedicated team of researchers. I would particularly like to acknowledge the debt that I owe to Julia Grant, Susan Brookes (now Susan Capella), Joan Chasin, Ruth Tibbitts, Caroline Yeeles, Yvonne Oakley and especially to John Clibbens. I would also like to thank my colleagues at Birkbeck College and Royal Holloway and Bedford New College—David Jones and Martyn Barrett—who collaborated on various parts of the research, and Sheila Gunzi, my postgraduate, who carried out one of the studies described in Chapter 7. I would also like to thank all the mothers and children who devoted such large amounts of time and enthusiasm to the various projects described here.

My research was made possible by several grants. The preliminary study described in Chapter 5 was carried out with funding from the Birkbeck College research committee. The second and third studies were supported by grant number COO 23 2136 from the Economic and Social Research Council and some of the examples of lexical development described in Chapter 4 came from another research project supported by the same agency (grant number ROOO 23 2037). The research on young deaf children was carried out with the aid of a grant from The Leverhulme Trust.

Finally, I must acknowledge the great debt that I owe to the many people with whom I have had stimulating discussions of the issues that

I consider here. I would especially like to thank the regular members of the Child Language Seminar whose enthusiasm for the study of child language has encouraged me to continue research in this area, and the Anglo-French Language, Concepts and Categorisation research group who stimulated me to think about the linguistic and philosophical implications of my research.

CHAPTER ONE

Language and the Environment: Some Evidence from Chomsky, Children and Chimpanzees

When thou dids't not, savage,
Know thine own meaning, but wouldst gabble like
A thing most brutish, I endowed thy purposes
With words that made them known.

The Tempest, Act 1, Scene 2

This book is about one of the most fundamental debates in language development, namely, the relationship between children's language development and their language experience. The historical roots of this debate go back to the writings of Locke, Berkley and Leibniz, but the starting point for recent psychological interest in this issue was an argument that began just over 30 years ago. This now famous debate—between the arch behaviourist B.F. Skinner and the linguist Noam Chomsky—centred on the opposition of two diametrically opposed accounts of language development and it was precipitated by the publication, in 1957, of Skinner's book, *Verbal behavior*.

One problem that often occurs when two disciplines collide is that there is a confusion about terminology. In the case of the debate that was begun when Chomsky took Skinner to task, there has been some confusion about the use of the terms "language acquisition" and "language development". You will see from the title of this book—and of this chapter—that I prefer the term "language development" and it is worth taking a moment to explain why.

Chomsky's main concern has always been with characterising the nature of linguistic knowledge and, in this respect, his preoccupations are much closer to those of a philosopher than a psychologist. He is thus interested in language acquisition, that is, in providing a theoretical account of the final state of knowledge of language that a child attains together with an account of the initial state of the child's linguistic knowledge and an account of the relationship between the initial and final states. Theoretical linguists like Chomsky are not interested in evidence about how real children actually use—and misuse—language, since they see this as providing no evidence either about the final state or the interim states that might exist as the child's knowledge evolves from the initial to the final state. This is because data about performance—the use of language on particular occasions—cannot provide direct evidence about language competence. What a child—or an adult—knows about language will only be one of many factors influencing language use.

Now, I firmly believe that an understanding of theories of language acquisition is important for psychologists who are attempting to account for language development. We need to take account of the insights that linguists and philosophers have had into the nature of language, even though we are concerned with the processes by which real children attain adult language competence. As such, our concern is with language development and with the changing processing abilities that are used as children master and deploy linguistic knowledge. It would be nice to think that, in the end, the processing considerations that are of interest to psychologists may also be of interest to those who theorise about language acquisition (see Harris & Davies, 1987, for a discussion of this point). But, for the moment at least, we must recognise that the agenda of the psychologist is significantly different from that of the theoretical linguist—or the philosopher—and so our main concern must be with language development and not language acquisition.

A HISTORICAL PERSPECTIVE: THE CHOMSKY–SKINNER DEBATE

You may well ask whether it is possible to say anything new or interesting about the profusely documented—and highly public—disagreement between Skinner and Chomsky. You might also sympathise with the view, expressed so elegantly by Bruner (borrowing from George Miller), that what we know from previous reviews of this debate "is that we shall make little progress if we adhere either to the impossible account of extreme empiricism or to the miraculous one of pure nativism" (Bruner, 1983b).

However, my reason for returning to the original Chomsky–Skinner debate is not only that I value a historical perspective (having very nearly become a medieval historian rather than a psychologist) but, more importantly, because I see the traditional opposition between nativist and empiricist accounts of language as having obscured the significance of the most important conclusions that have emerged from recent studies of the relationship between language development and language experience. This is because any suggestion that language development might be influenced by linguistic input is sometimes mistakenly seen as returning to an empiricist position that was demolished long ago.

It is is also worth noting that, over the intervening years since his original attack on Skinner, Chomsky has amplified his views on the nature of language acquisition in a series of influential monographs culminating in *Knowledge of language* (Chomsky, 1986). Indeed, some might argue that Chomsky had radically changed his view of language and there are interesting questions to be raised about differences between the picture of acquisition that Chomsky paints at various points (see, for example, Botha, 1989; Harris & Davies, 1987). It is, nevertheless, clear that the basis of Chomsky's opposition to a behaviourist account of language learning remains essentially unchanged.

Language and Operant Conditioning

One way to understand what it is that Chomsky still finds so objectionable in Skinner's account of language development is to consider Chomsky's rejection of the term "learning" as a description of the processes that occur when a child develops mastery of his/her native language. Skinner's claim was that children "learn" language through operant conditioning. In Skinner's view, language learning involved processes that were essentially similar to those used when laboratory animals are trained to make simple responses such as pushing a lever—in the case of a rat—or pecking at a disk—in the case of a pigeon. The essence of operant conditioning (see Walker, 1984, for a detailed account) is that it merely involves the attachment of a response to a stimulus through the use of carefully controlled reinforcement. It is an entirely passive process and does not involve any active learning by the organism in whom the conditioning occurs.

Skinner's claim in *Verbal behavior* is that children receive reinforcement for uttering certain sounds. The reinforcement is not food or water—as for a rat or pigeon—but rather parental encouragement and approval. Skinner provides some examples of how the conditioning of children's verbal behaviour might occur:

> In all verbal behavior under stimulus control there are three important events to be taken into account: a stimulus, a response and a reinforcement. These are contingent upon each other .... The three term contingency ... is exemplified when, in the presence of a doll, a child frequently achieves some sort of generalized reinforcement by saying *doll* (Skinner, 1957, p.81).

> The child first hears *No!* as the occasion upon which some current activity must be stopped if positive reinforcement is to be received or aversive stimulation avoided. When the child later engages in the same activity, he recreates an occasion upon which the response *No!* is strong. Upon such occasions he is especially likely to receive a generalised reinforcement for the verbal response (Skinner, 1957, p.323).

Note that both these examples concern the child learning to say single words although there are some significant differences between them. In the first case—which Skinner describes as a "tact"—the child is learning to use a word that refers to an object in the world. In the second case—that of a "mand"—the child is learning to produce a word that is associated with the cessation of a behaviour. Interestingly, as we will see in Chapter 6, Skinner's intuition about the differences between these two cases has correlates in recent research into lexical development: The acquisition of a "mand" and a "tact" do present the child with somewhat different problems. What is fundamentally flawed, however, is the claim that the acquisition of either kind of lexical item is mediated by reinforcement in the way that Skinner claims.

The rejection of the critical role of reinforcement in language acquisition formed a central part of Chomsky's attack on Skinner. Another major concern of Chomsky's critique was Skinner's failure to take account of the central role of syntactic knowledge in language competence.

There has been some confusion about Skinner's views on syntax and, in many ways, they are much more sophisticated than is often claimed. In the light of some of the caricatures that have been drawn, it is interesting to note that Skinner does make some attempt to grapple with the problem of accounting for a speaker's capacity to produce novel utterances, albeit that the attempt is not successful. At least Skinner was aware that it was a feature of language use that had to be accounted for. Here is a flavour of the Skinnerian account of how novel utterances might be produced by using "partially conditioned frames". You may be surprised by it, although I doubt that you will find it convincing:

> Having responded to many pairs of objects with behaviour such as *the hat and the shoe* and *the gun and the hat*, the speaker may make the response *the boy and the bicycle* on a novel occasion. If he has acquired a series of responses such as *the boy's gun*, *the boy's shoe* and *the boy's hat*, we may suppose that the partial frame *the boy's_____* is available for a recombination with other responses. The first time the boy acquires a bicycle, the speaker can compose a new unit *the boy's bicycle* (Skinner, 1957, p.336).

The Nativist Response

Chomsky was singularly unimpressed by Skinner's notion of "frames" and much of his attack centred on what he saw as Skinner's inability to account for syntactic productivity. Chomsky's main objection to the claim that language could be "learned" through operant conditioning was that the essence of knowing a language is acquiring knowledge that allows a speaker to produce and understand utterances that he/she has never heard before. In other words, whereas for Skinner the question of linguistic productivity was a secondary one, for Chomsky it lay at the heart of accounting for language acquisition. Acquiring a language involved the acquisition of a body of knowledge and, in Chomsky's view, such knowledge was best described by a set of rules (Chomsky, 1965) or, in more recent formulations (Chomsky, 1986), by a set of principles and parameters. These rules or principles are highly abstract so that, even if a child were to be provided only with examples of grammatically correct speech, it would still be impossible for the child to extract such rules solely from experience (see the discussion of the "poverty of the stimulus" in Chapter 2).

As is well known, Chomsky's solution to this fundamental problem that experience could never be sufficient for language acquisition was to posit the existence of a powerful innate device that would lead the child to knowledge of language on the basis of minimal linguistic exposure. According to Chomsky, this device is present only in the human brain and it endows human offspring with a unique ability to acquire language.

As I have already pointed out, Chomsky's main objection to Skinner's account of language development centred round the impossibility of presenting an empiricist account of syntactic development. However, some of the objections that Chomsky originally raised in 1959—and has repeated on numerous occasions—can be seen as applying to lexical development. Chief among these is the assertion that children are not given the kind of systematic and repeated reinforcement that operant conditioning requires. Stimulus, response and reinforcement have to occur over and over again for even simple learning to take place.

Chomsky's claim was that, far from receiving systematic reinforcement, children's exposure to language is so unsystematic that their language experience does not even serve as a good model of correct adult usage. Note, again, that this is really a point about the inadequacy of adult language as a model for the acquisition of syntax.

Chomsky's major objection to a behaviourist account of language is not, however, predicated upon his claims about the grammatical inadequacies of the language that the child hears. (As we will see in Chapter 2, there has been much debate about the accuracy of Chomsky's claims about the unsystematic nature of adult speech to children.) Pushed to its limit, Chomsky's argument is that, *even with optimal linguistic input*, it would still be impossible for the child to acquire knowledge of language—particularly knowledge of syntax—on the basis of general learning principles. The attainment of such knowledge is only possible because the child possesses an innate, language-specific, mechanism—a language acquisition device.

The Analogy with Physical Growth

Chomsky's favourite analogy for the operation of the innate language acquisition device (LAD) is with the child's physical growth. He claims that, far from involving a process of learning, language develops—or is "acquired"—in much the same way that arms and legs grow or that physical changes occur at puberty. A programme for development is laid down at birth and only a minimal contribution from the environment is required:

> ... language is only in the most marginal sense taught and that teaching
> is in no sense essential to the acquisition of language. In a certain sense
> I think we might even go on and say that language is not even learned
> ... It seems to me that, if we want a reasonable metaphor, we should talk
> about growth. Language seems to me to grow in the mind rather as
> familiar physical systems of the body grow. We begin our interchange
> with the world with our minds in a particular genetically determined
> state. Through interaction with experience—with everything around
> us—this state changes until it reaches a mature state we call a state of
> knowledge of language ... this series of changes seems to me analogous
> to the growth of organs (Chomsky, 1979).

Although this often-quoted analogy between the development of language and the course of puberty is a very powerful one, there is a significant way in which the analogy is misleading. This is evidenced by the fact that developing a precise formulation of the role of the environment is much more difficult than it is in the case of physical development.

The pattern of hormonal and corresponding physical changes that will occur in a child at puberty is genetically determined. The environment—particularly nutrition—may affect the age at which a child enters puberty, but it will not influence the kind of changes that occur. As Fodor (1983) has pointed out, however, this is not the case with language. The particular language that a child hears will affect the content of language development. The language environment provides data or evidence in favour of one language hypothesis—or parameter setting—rather than another (for a detailed discussion of this point, see Atkinson, 1987; Harris & Davies, 1987). So, clearly, there is a relationship between language development and the linguistic environment—what Fodor calls a "content relation"—that is different in kind from that between physical development and the physical environment, and it is to this extent that Chomsky's analogy is misleading. Its purpose is to draw a vivid contrast between the view that language development is innately determined and the view that language development can be explained in terms of conditioning principles operating upon language experience. But we should remember that the analogy ought not to be pushed too far.

LEXICAL AND SYNTACTIC DEVELOPMENT

Another point that we should bear in mind about the traditional opposition of nativist and empiricist views of language is that it is mistaken to consider language as an indivisible entity when considering the putative influence of the environment.

It is true that there are general arguments to be made about the role of the environment in language development, but there are also somewhat different points to be made about lexical development and grammatical development. As we saw, Chomsky's main theoretical concern has been with grammar and, particularly, syntax. His main objection to an environmentally driven account of language development is that it cannot account for the child's ability to acquire syntactic productivity.

It is certainly arguable that the capacity to acquire syntax lies at the heart of language development. But in order for syntactic knowledge to be utilised, children also have to acquire a vocabulary. Some of the most recent studies of chimpanzees learning sign language suggest that, although the capacity for syntax is uniquely human, chimpanzees, as well as children, may be able to acquire a lexicon and also to combine signs in simple multi-word utterances.[1] If this is the case, there may be good reasons for considering that the acquisition of a lexicon and the acquisition of syntax should be seen in a somewhat different light from the standpoint of the nativist–empiricist debate. Since this issue has a direct bearing on some of the evidence that I will be considering later in this book, I want to spend a little time on a digression into the implications of recent research on the symbolic capacity of chimpanzees.

The Symbolic Capacities of Chimpanzees

The capacity for language acquisition in apes has been the focus of a large number of research projects over the last 20 years. The most well known of these are the studies of the chimpanzees, Washoe (Gardner & Gardner, 1971, 1974) and Nim (Terrace, 1979, 1985), who were trained to produce signs from American Sign Language (ASL), and the studies carried out by Premack, in which chimpanzees were trained to use an artificial language via a keyboard (see Premack, 1986, for an overview).

There has been considerable disagreement about the conclusions that can be drawn from these studies. Some authors (e.g. Fouts, 1972) have argued that chimpanzees show a considerable capacity both for symbolic representation and syntactic productivity. Others (notably Petitto & Seidenberg—see Petitto & Seidenberg, 1979; Seidenberg & Petitto, 1979) have been dismissive of such claims, arguing that the chimpanzee's use of signs is little more than an impressive example of conditioning. Interestingly, Premack appears to have changed his own view about the potential linguistic competence of apes and in his recent book (Premack, 1986) concludes that apes cannot be turned into children even with the most extensive language training (see Walker, 1987, for a discussion of this point).

Recently, the debate about the linguistic capacities of apes was reawakened by reports of the performance of a young male pygmy chimpanzee, Kanzi. The chimpanzees used in previous studies were common chimpanzees (*Pan troglodytes*) and comparative studies suggest that the social-communicative repertoire of the pygmy chimpanzee (*Pan paniscus*) is more complex. There is also some evidence that the pygmy chimpanzee is more intelligent than the common chimp.

Kanzi was observed by Savage-Rumbaugh (Savage-Rumbaugh et al., 1986), who had previously trained the chimpanzees, Austin and Sherman (Savage-Rumbaugh, 1986). Unlike Washoe and Nim, Austin and Sherman were trained to communicate through a keyboard which activated geometric symbols.

Savage-Rumbaugh begins her account of Kanzi's performance by describing the limitations of the linguistic achievements of Austin and Sherman. She notes that they had to be given explicit training to go beyond the use of a particular visual symbol in response to a particular context to the use of that symbol to refer to objects and activities in a variety of situations.

> The weight of the evidence to date suggests that apes tend to learn symbols in an associational manner, and they need explicit training in order to enable them to use symbols referentially. ... However, once they are given such training, their symbol usage begins to take on an increasingly representational character until finally they are able to use symbols to convey intended actions (Savage-Rumbaugh et al., 1986, p.213).

The fact that common chimpanzees do not appear to progress spontaneously towards the referential use of symbols makes them significantly different from children. Their comprehension of words also appears to be inferior in that it is situationally linked and heavily dependent upon contextual cues.

The linguistic abilities shown by Kanzi, however, appear to be a significant advance in both these areas. Kanzi's exposure to visual symbols was also unusual in that he learned to use the symbol keyboard spontaneously rather than in special training sessions. He had an opportunity to do so because he was able to observe the use of the visual symbol keyboard by his mother, Matata, who had been the subject of an earlier study (Savage-Rumbaugh & Wilkerson, 1978). When it became clear that Kanzi had learned the symbols on the keyboard, he was provided with a pointing board that could be taken outside the laboratory. The board contained photographs of the symbols on the keyboard—lexigrams—and a particular symbol was selected by pointing.

As I have already mentioned, Kanzi—and his sister, Mulika—did not receive formal training in symbol use. In particular, their acquisition of lexigrams was not systematically reinforced through the presentation of food rewards:

> ... people modelled symbol use during their communications with each other and with the chimpanzees. During all daily activities (playing, eating, resting, travelling in the woods, etc.) people commented on and emphasized their activities both vocally and visually by pointing to the appropriate lexigrams on the keyboard. For example, if they were

engaged in a tickling bout, the teacher would comment "(teacher's name) tickle Kanzi" both via the keyboard and vocally (Savage-Rumbaugh et al., 1986, p.216).

Kanzi was credited with the acquisition of a lexigram only if he spontaneously produced the item on at least nine occasions and also provided unambiguous evidence that he was using it appropriately, for example, by taking one of this teachers to the location indicated by the lexigram. At the end of the observation period, Kanzi was also subjected to stringent testing for comprehension of all the items in his production vocabulary.

A Comparison of Child and Chimpanzee

The use of such strict criteria in the judgement of Kanzi's language development allows us to place considerable faith in Savage-Rumbaugh's reports of Kanzi's progress. In particular, it is of considerable significance that Kanzi's comprehension was tested because evidence about production alone is inconclusive. We need clear evidence of understanding in order to be certain that a chimp—or a child—has acquired a symbol.

Kanzi's comprehension performance was impressive not least because there was a regular pattern to his acquisition of individual symbols, which mirrors that found in children. Kanzi comprehended lexigrams *before* he produced them. Indeed, he often comprehended both the spoken English word and the lexigram before using the latter in production. For example, Kanzi began to show signs of understanding the word "strawberries" and he would rush over to the strawberry patch when the word was mentioned. Later, the strawberry lexigram was added to Kanzi's keyboard and he learned to use it to request a strawberry to eat, to ask to travel to the strawberry patch and also when shown a picture of strawberries.

Seidenberg and Petitto (1987) have been very dismissive of Kanzi's achievements. They have argued that Kanzi's lexigram use was merely instrumental and did not reflect genuine symbol use of the kind that is evidenced by the child acquiring language:

> The generalization of the accounts for Kanzi's behavior is not that lexigrams function as words or symbols but rather that he adapts in a problem-solving manner to the experimental condition that confronts him. His behavior differs significantly depending upon the context, which would not be expected if in fact he knew that lexigrams were symbols for particular types of object (Seidenberg & Petitto, 1987, p.282).

The main evidence that Seidenberg and Petitto provide for this view centres on their claim that Kanzi's production of lexigrams violates the natural categories of object and event in a way that young children's word use does not. For example, Kanzi used "strawberry" not only in response to the sight of strawberries or a picture of strawberries but also as a request for a strawberry to eat and as a request to travel to the area where the strawberries grew. Seidenberg and Petitto claim that children's word use does not operate in such an unprincipled fashion. They cite as evidence an experiment by Markman and Hutchinson (1984) in which young children were taught a novel word (e.g. dax) in conjunction with a picture (e.g. COW). They were then shown two further pictures and asked to pick out another instance of the same category by finding "another kind of dax". Given a choice between a thematically related item (e.g. cow – MILK) or a taxonomically related item (e.g. cow – PIG), the children showed a consistent preference for the taxonomically related item. Significantly, the children did not show this pattern if they were merely shown the first picture and then asked to find "another one", suggesting that it was the use of a word that was constraining the picture choice.

Both Savage-Rumbaugh (1987) and Nelson (1987) have convincingly argued that Seidenberg and Petitto's claims both underestimate Kanzi's achievements and overestimate the lexical accomplishments of young children. One highly significant fact about the Markman and Hutchinson experiments that Seidenberg and Petitto ignore is that they were carried out with pre-school children whose average age was 4 years. In other words, these were children whose language development was highly sophisticated. They were not—like Kanzi—at the initial stage of vocabulary learning, so the comparison is unfair. And if we actually consider what children's *early* word use is like, it is common to find the use of one word both to label an object and as a request to be taken to or given that object. Indeed, a recent study by Dromi (1986) found that 16% of the words used by her daughter in the single-word period were indeterminate in that they crossed adult boundaries. For example, the word "hot" was used both as a name for ovens and heaters and for the property of being either hot or cold.

Language as a Distinctive Human Ability

I find it somewhat surprising that claims about the symbolic capacity of chimpanzees should be so controversial. Presumably the vehemence of the opposition to the claims of Savage-Rumbaugh and others stems from a wish to support the view that "language is unique to the human species". But this is not the only strongly nativist view that could be defended. For example, it might be the case that chimpanzees—and *a fortiori* pygmy chimpanzees—are capable of representing the perceptual world by means of symbols and so are capable of learning to use signs to represent a limited range of states in the world. But if this were the case, it would be very far indeed from claiming that chimps are capable of acquiring language, since this involves the mastery of syntax and the capacity to acquire signs that represent abstract concepts. It would still be possible to argue that these essential aspects of language remain the exclusive province of human beings.

If evolution occurs by a process of cumulative selection involving tiny steps, then it seems highly likely that our closest ancestor might have developed a capacity that is essential, but far from sufficient, for language. As Dawkins (1986) has pointed out, there is a tendency to exaggerate the special status of human beings, since our perspective is blurred by the fact that the intermediates between humans and chimps are all dead. He paints a vivid picture of the legal, moral and ethical problems that would arise if such intermediates existed:

> The last common ancestor of humans and chimps lived perhaps as recently as five million years ago, definitely more recently than the common ancestor of chimps and orang-utans. ... Chimpanzees and we share more than 99 per cent of our genes. If, in various forgotten islands around the world, survivors of all the intermediates back to the chimp/human common ancestor were discovered, who can doubt that our laws and moral conventions would be profoundly affected? ... Anybody who thinks that there is something obvious and self-evident about human "rights" should reflect that it is just sheer luck that these embarrassing intermediates happen not to have survived (Dawkins, 1986, p.263).

It seems to me that a similar question about the uniqueness of language might also arise if we were more aware of the genetic continuity between us and chimps. We might be forced to question the assumption that the division between the human and chimpanzee capacity for language is all-or-none. But since the probability of discovering such intermediates is remote, we must be content with keeping an open mind about the extent to which chimps can engage in symbolic communication. If we accept, for the moment, that the claims about Kanzi's abilities are correct, then we can consider the possibility that the processes involved in syntactic development may be different from those involved in lexical development. In particular, we can explore the hypothesis that, although the course of syntactic development may largely proceed according to innate principles, the child's linguistic environment has a significant influence upon lexical development and *a fortiori* upon early lexical development.

LANGUAGE AND EXPERIENCE: AN INTERACTIONIST VIEW

So far I have suggested that the child's linguistic environment may have a particularly important role to play in the early stages of language development. In the following chapters, I will review the evidence from a number of studies that have attempted to explore the relationship between the language addressed to the child and the child's own language development; and I will consider whether there is empirical evidence for the hypothesis that I have outlined.

It is essential to be clear at the outset what would constitute evidence for the view that I am attempting to support. One important line of evidence concerns the relationship between the rate at which children develop language and the kind of linguistic input that they receive. If early language development is affected by linguistic input, then one would expect to find evidence that there is a relationship between the two. However, as I will go on to show in the following chapters, there are no reasons to suppose that this relationship is a simple one, or one that could be detected by casual inspection.

Let me try to make this point clear. We need to remember that, as with all cognitive development, the course of language development will be the outcome of an interaction between the child's own processing abilities and experience. Linguistic data—however transparent—will never be sufficient for language development. My cats are daily exposed to ideal linguistic data of the kind I describe in Chapters 5 and 7, but so far their linguistic progress has been negligible. (They can understand no more than half a dozen words presented in a limited range of contexts.) So what is at issue is more a question of necessity than one of sufficiency. In other words, I am not attempting to defend the position that language experience is sufficient for language development, but rather the view that such experience is necessary.

However, this latter view in its barest form is not interesting, since all theorists agree that language experience is necessary for development to occur. Even the most extreme nativist position recognises that some linguistic data are required, since the particular language that a child is to learn cannot be genetically determined. As Landau and Gleitman (1985, p.1) put it:

> No disagreement arises, then, about the necessity for extralinguistic experience. But despite this agreement, ... theorists ... vary considerably

in their conceptions of how language is attained in the young child. Their disagreements have to do with the *sufficiency* of experience for learning a language. Exactly how is the relevant external experience to be internally represented? How can anyone *use* this experience to learn a language?

What I will argue in this book is that certain features of the child's language experience facilitate language development. That is, their presence makes the early stages of language development easier for the young child. The evidence for this claim—which I set out in more detail in Chapter 4—comes from a variety of sources which I discuss in the following chapters.

NOTE

1.   I am assuming here that the early stages of multi-word speech—particularly two- and three-word utterances—are best thought of as pre-syntactic.

CHAPTER TWO

Language Development and Adult Speech

The last two decades have witnessed considerable fluctuations in optimism about the possibility of discovering links between adult speech and children's language development. I use the word "optimism" advisedly because researchers in this area have traditionally been divided into those for whom "optimism" constituted the view that much of language development could be explained in terms of linguistic input and those among whom the opposite view prevailed.

The earlier research in this area has already been reviewed at length (see Snow, 1977; Harris & Coltheart, 1986) and so I want to concentrate in this chapter upon some of the more recent findings. However, as there is a clear continuity between the earlier and more recent research, I will begin by summarising some of the main findings that emerged from studies in the 1970s and early 1980s.

EARLY STUDIES OF ADULT SPEECH TO CHILDREN

The Degeneracy of the Stimulus

Child language researchers' original interest in the speech that adults use to children was prompted by Chomsky's observation that the language children hear is typically incomplete and ungrammatical. This is a claim that Chomsky has made at various times and in various guises, most influentially in *Aspects of the theory of syntax* (Chomsky, 1965). More recently, Chomsky (1980) has fleshed out his claims about the nature of linguistic experience and has drawn an important distinction between *the degeneracy of the stimulus* and *the poverty of the stimulus*.

What Chomsky means by the "degeneracy" of the language that children hear is that spoken language—much more than written language—contains expressions that are not well formed. Such ill-formedness—what a native speaker would recognise as ungrammaticality—arises because of such phenomena as slips of the tongue, pauses, false starts, inconsistent use of number and tense, and so on. According to Chomsky, the fact that errors of this kind occur in adult speech means that the language children hear cannot provide an accurate guide as to what is grammatically correct in a given language.

By contrast with the claim that spoken language contains errors, the idea behind the "poverty of the stimulus" is that neither spoken nor written language—even if completely error-free—could ever provide evidence for certain properties and principles of the language that children acquire. Putting this another way, Chomsky's claim here is that the underlying properties and principles of language are so abstract that a child could not deduce them merely from a systematic analysis of linguistic input. (Note the claim is not that the underlying rules—or principles—could never by deduced by anyone, otherwise theoretical linguistics would be impossible!)

As I will show in a moment, the distinction between these two types of putative inadequacy in linguistic input has sometimes been blurred. It is important to remember that, even if Chomsky's claims about the *degeneracy* of the stimulus prove to be incorrect, it does not follow that Chomsky's arguments about the limitations of linguistic input as a basis for language learning can be dismissed unless it can be shown that the same is true of his claim about the *poverty* of the stimulus. Following Chomsky's distinction, there are thus two distinct questions about adult speech to children for child language researchers to consider: What is the nature of adult speech to children and can such speech provide a *sufficient* basis for the development of language mastery? In practice, however, the question of the sufficiency of linguistic input is one that has not been directly addressed by the great majority of researchers who have studied adult speech to children. Their main issue of concern has been whether or not the speech that children hear has an influence upon language development.

The Emergence of Motherese

The first findings to emerge from studies of adult speech to children were remarkably consistent. They showed that adult speech—or, more specifically, maternal speech, since it was this that was invariably the object of study—had certain characteristics that distinguished it from speech to other adults. These characteristics were in essence simplicity, brevity and redundancy.

The first published study to describe the properties of what rapidly became known as "motherese" was that of Snow (1972). Snow's study highlighted the syntactic simplification of motherese and the short utterances that it contained. She also noted that the shortness and syntactic simplicity of maternal utterances meant that the language that children heard was invariably grammatical—since ungrammaticality tends to increase as a function of complexity—and also highly repetitive.

Snow's study also revealed that mothers spoke differently to children of different ages. She compared their speech to 2-year-old and 10-year-old children and found that mothers used longer and syntactically more complex utterances to the older children.

These findings were confirmed by many other studies, including those of Phillips (1973), who found that motherese contained fewer verbs, modifiers and function words than normal speech, and Cross (1977, 1978), who argued that the gradually increasing complexity of motherese arose, in part, as a response to the linguistic feedback about developing comprehension and production that was provided by the child.

Subsequent studies were aimed at investigating two issues that arose from the identification of a unique speech register for addressing children. One concerned the factors that were responsible for the fine-tuning of motherese to children of varying ages and linguistic abilities. The second concerned the much thornier question of whether motherese had a function as an ideal teaching language for the child who was attempting to master language.

As in many areas of developmental psychology, the answer to the first question about the determinants of motherese was that a multi-factor account seemed to provide the best explanation. A study by Cross, Johnson-Morris and Nienhuys (1980) of maternal speech to hearing and hearing-impaired children revealed that three different factors contributed to the linguistic complexity of motherese. The child's own level of language comprehension had the greatest influence on maternal speech, but a mother's expectations about her child's linguistic potential were also important, as was the child's more general level of communicative competence.

The fact that the way an individual mother talks to a child is significantly determined by the child's own linguistic ability, presents an obvious problem when it comes to answering questions about the relationship between maternal speech and children's language development. We would expect there to be a relationship between maternal speech and child language just because mothers are responsive to the linguistic abilities of their children. Thus it would be expected that the mother of a child with relatively sophisticated language comprehension would use more complex language than the mother of a child with less advanced comprehension. So merely showing that maternal speech and child speech are related does not in itself demonstrate that the way mothers talk actually has an influence upon their children's language development.

The problem of teasing apart cause and effect was one that haunted the studies of motherese that were carried out in the 1980s. Another concern that was expressed with increasing frequency was whether studies that concentrated exclusively on mothers, and on the child-rearing environment of westernised cultures, could provide a universal picture of the linguistic input that children receive. This is an issue that I will return to in the final chapter.

LATER STUDIES OF ADULT SPEECH
TO CHILDREN

The Motherese Hypothesis

The crux of the argument about the relationship between maternal speech and child language development—and associated methodological problems—can best be illustrated by examining the debate that took place between Newport, Gleitman and Gleitman on the one hand, and Furrow, Nelson and Benedict on the other. These two groups of investigators occupied significantly different positions with respect to what became known as "the Motherese Hypothesis". In essence, Furrow et al. were supporters of the hypothesis which claimed that the special properties of maternal speech—notably its simplicity—play a *causal* (and necessary) role in language development: Newport et al. argued that motherese did not determine language development in general but had only a marginal effect in influencing the speed with which certain morpho-syntactic items were learned.

The debate was instigated by a major study carried out by Newport, Gleitman and Gleitman (1977), which investigated the relationship between mothers' speech and children's language growth in the second year of life. The authors analysed data from two recordings of mother–daughter dyads made 6 months apart and examined correlations between various measures of mothers' speech in the first session and measures of development in the children's speech from the first to the second session. A number of different aspects of children's language development were assessed and these varied from morpho-syntactic developments (e.g. noun inflections and auxiliaries) to increases in the number of semantic relations and grammatical functions that were expressed.

An important methodological aspect of the Newport et al. study was that the age and language competence of the children at the first session was partialled out of their analysis. Their aim in so doing was to provide a measure of the effects of mothers' speech upon children's language development that was independent of the children's age or linguistic ability. Their main conclusion was that, once allowance had been made for the initial language competence of the children, the influence of maternal speech was highly circumscribed: the only aspects of language development that proved to be related to maternal speech involved a strictly limited set of morpho-syntactic items, notably auxiliaries.

Furrow, Nelson and Benedict (1979) raised various objections to the Newport et al. study. Their main criticism hinged on what they saw as the underlying assumption of the statistical treatment of data by Newport et al., namely that the effects of motherese would be uniform across all ages and stages of language development. Such an assumption is inherent in the use of the majority of correlational analyses which assume linearity of effects (see Chapter 4 for a more detailed discussion of this point).

Furrow et al. set out to develop a methodology that did not make what they described as "the unwarranted assumptions of prior studies". Their solution to the problems of non-linearity in the relationship between child language and maternal speech was to match both the age and stage of language development of children at the time that the sample of maternal speech was taken. Unfortunately, the "stage" selected for matching was Brown's (1973) Early Stage I, which spans the single-word period and the start of multi-word combinations.

The most commonly used measure of children's language is MLU or mean length of utterance. This measure is derived by taking a sample of the child's spontaneous speech and working out the average length of an utterance.[1] When children first start to combine words, their MLU begins to increase beyond 1. However, as we will see in Chapter 6, there are considerable developments within the single-word period. There are also differences at the point in vocabulary development at which children first begin to combine words. Some children do not begin combining until they have a vocabulary of 100 or more words, whereas others may start to combine words when they know only a few. Thus a group of children, all of whom have a MLU of one of just over 1, may have greatly differing lexical knowledge.

Apart from the differences in initial matching of subjects, the methodology of the Furrow et al. study was essentially the same as that of Newport et al. Speech samples were obtained from seven mother–child dyads when the children were 1:6 to 2:3 years old.[2] One hundred utterances of maternal speech were analysed according to a number of semantic and syntactic categories. The syntactic measures were extensive and included frequency of use of such forms as wh-questions, yes/no questions (requiring the child to reply either yes/no), tag questions, declaratives and imperatives, past and future tenses, negatives and prepositions. The analyses of the children's speech were exclusively syntactic and concentrated on the length and complexity of utterances.

Furrow et al. found a number of significant relationships between maternal speech and children's language at the second session. (Since the children had been matched for initial language level, it was not necessary to take a measure of language change from the first to second sessions.) Mothers' speech to their children during the first session was related to four different measures[3] of children's language at the second session, 9 months later. The pattern of results was complex but the measures of maternal speech that were most highly associated with complexity of child speech were frequency of yes/no questions, pronouns, verbs and copulas. The number of words used by the mothers in 100 utterances (which is a measure of their utterance length) was also correlated with child speech at the second session.

Only one of these relationships was a positive one, that is, associated with greater language development by the end of the study. In view of the earlier finding of Newport et al. (1977), the reader may not be surprised to learn that there were positive correlations between maternal use of yes/no questions and all measures of child speech. However, child language development was *negatively* correlated with all the other measures of maternal speech mentioned above—frequency of pronouns, verbs and copulas and the number of words used by the mothers in 100 utterances.

One additional aspect of the Furrow et al. study was that they considered the children's relative abilities in language comprehension as well as language production. Using data from Benedict (unpublished), it was possible to rank order the seven children according to their ability to respond to a number of spoken commands at the beginning of the study. Comprehension skills proved to be significantly correlated with mothers' MLU at the first session and also with production at the end of the study.

The main conclusion drawn by Furrow et al. from their findings was that aspects of maternal speech that are associated with *simplicity* of communicative style are positively related to language growth, whereas use of a more complex style is associated with slower development. Towards the end of their article, the authors went so far as to suggest that "complexities in mothers' speech hindered language development". The basis for their conclusion was that the measures that were negatively correlated with child speech—use of pronouns, verbs and the copula —are all indications of utterance complexity.

I am by no means convinced that the basis of the Furrow et al. claims about the complexity of maternal speech is correct but, as these findings are re-examined in the next section, I want to concentrate on another issue that gives cause for concern. This is the relationship between maternal language and the children's comprehension at the start of the study. As I noted earlier in the chapter, maternal speech is influenced by a number of factors. The study by Cross et al. (1980) suggests that the child's own level of language comprehension has the greatest influence on maternal speech. In the Furrow et al. study, it was also the case that language comprehension was highly related to language production several months later. (A similar finding has recently emerged from a much more extensive study of children of the same age carried out by Bates, Bretherton and Snyder, 1988.) It is, therefore, at least possible that the child's developing comprehension may have been the main factor linking maternal speech at the start of the study to the child's language production 9 months later. In other words, the complexity of maternal speech was being influenced by the child's level of comprehension, which was also a good predictor of—and major influence upon—the level of language production some months later. This problem was highlighted by Gleitman, Newport and Gleitman (1984) in their response to the Furrow et al. paper.

Reinterpreting the Motherese Hypothesis

The paper by Gleitman et al. (1984) set out to resolve the conflicting results that had emerged from the studies of Newport et al. (1977) and Furrow et al. (1979). As we have seen, the major difference between the two studies lay not in their positive findings but in their negative ones. There was also a methodological difference in that the Newport et al. study had used a measure of language change from the first observation session to the second (language at t_2 – language at t_1), while Furrow et al. had matched the children for age and MLU at the first session and had considered only language ability at the second session. It will be remembered that Furrow et al. adopted this method because they argued that it was misleading to compare changes in the language ability of children who were at different ages and stages of development.

Gleitman et al. (1984) pointed out that their method of partial correlation (taking account of age and initial language ability) had allowed them to equate the children in their sample statistically. However, they did accept the criticism made by Furrow et al. that, because they had used subjects who varied in age by more than 1 year, they had compared children who were going through different stages of language development. Accordingly, in their 1984 paper, Gleitman et al. re-analysed the data grouping their original subjects according to chronological age and applied the same measures as Furrow et al. This grouping reduced the sample to two groups of six children.

The new analyses produced some significant correlations between maternal speech and child language growth. However, conscious of the fact that in a large matrix some correlations will be significant purely by chance, Gleitman et al. carried out a "split half" analysis in which separate correlations were computed for each measure on each half of the data. The results were treated as significant only if the results on the two halves of the analysis were comparable (and similar to the overall result). With this more rigorous statistical methodology, correlations between simplicity of maternal speech and language growth disappeared; and further correlations became insignificant when the same "split half" technique was applied to the partial correlations that took account of the child's initial age and language ability.

Overall, the Gleitman et al. study found very few reliably significant correlations. Interestingly, the highest correlation of 0.99 was between maternal *unintelligibility* and growth in the child's use of verbs per utterance. The authors chose to interpret this as an artefact of their data—a sensible decision—but this finding vividly illustrates the great difficulty of interpreting the theoretical significance of correlations.

A number of more plausible correlations occurred for the group of younger children (ranging in age from 18 to 21 months and comparable to the Furrow et al. subjects). There was a positive correlation between maternal use of declaratives and the child's use of verbs per utterance, and a negative correlation between maternal repetition and growth in both MLU and use of auxiliaries. The growth in the children's use of auxiliary verbs was correlated with maternal use of expansions, maternal MLU, number of clauses per utterance and frequency of interjections (the latter also being associated with growth in MLU). In the older group (age range 24–27 months), only one measure of maternal speech produced significant correlations—use of yes/no questions was related to growth in both MLU and use of auxiliaries.

As the reader may have noted, the main finding emerging from the elaborate analyses of Gleitman et al. was that auxiliary development showed the strongest relationship to maternal speech. The precise correlations were different for the two age groups with more general measures of maternal style being involved for the younger children and use of yes/no questions being implicated for the older children.

The finding that development in the use of auxiliaries is correlated with various measures of maternal speech has proved to be a persistent one, as we will see in the next section. However, before leaving the Gleitman et al. study, it is worth noting one particularly provocative point that they raise in their discussion. This concerns the conclusion of the Furrow et al. paper, that it is syntactic *simplicity* of maternal speech that facilitates language development. What Gleitman et al. suggest is that it may be mothers who produce a greater range of syntactically different kinds of utterance who are providing the most useful linguistic data for their children. Their argument (which is derived from the work of learning theorists such as Wexler and Culicover, 1980) is essentially that mastery of a complex syntactic system, which contains many and varied structures, will best be served by data that mirror this range.

I think that there is a lot of truth in this claim and a close analysis of recent findings on the development of the auxiliary (see Richards, 1990) suggests that the child's mastery of these forms is related in a very indirect way to their appearance in maternal speech. It is by no means the case that what best predicts the rate of auxiliary development is the frequency with which adults use these forms in simple sentences.

The Bristol Longitudinal Study of Language Development

At the same time as research was being carried out in the United States, another study to examine the complexities of the relationship between maternal speech and children's language development was being carried out in Bristol by Wells and his co-workers (Ellis & Wells, 1980; Barnes, Gutfreund, Satterly & Wells, 1983; Wells, 1981). The Bristol study was considerably more extensive than either of the American studies described in the two previous sections, with two cohorts of children being followed for several years. The younger cohort consisted of 64 children who were observed between the ages of 15 and 42 months at 3-monthly intervals.

The methodology of the Bristol study was unusual in that samples of speech addressed to the children were collected in the home using a radio microphone worn by the child that was turned on and off remotely for 90-sec periods. The microphone picked up all the speech that was directed to the child and this included input from a variety of adults. The speech samples were taken at approximately 20-min intervals throughout the day so that a wide range of contexts was included. Detailed contextual information was obtained the same evening by re-playing the tape to the parents and asking them about the situations in which the speech had been recorded. The extensive database of the Bristol study has been analysed in a series of papers. For present purposes, the most interesting analyses are those of Ellis and Wells (1980), Barnes et al. (1983) and Richards (1990).

In the Ellis and Wells analysis, the children were subdivided into three groups according to their rate of language development. In all three groups, the children had an MLU of 1.5 at the start of observation but they attained an MLU of 3.5 at different ages. The most precocious group—the Early Fast Developers (EFD)—were between 18 and 21 months when their MLU reached 1.5 and took 6 months or less to attain an MLU of 3.5. The Late Fast Developers (LFD) also took 6 months or less to progress from an MLU of 1.5 to one of 3.5, but they were, on average, 6 months older when they reached the first of these points (and so also 6 months older when they attained the second point). The Slow Developers (SD) all took 12 months or longer to progress from an MLU of 1.5 to one of 3.5.

Several different measures of the children's speech were taken at the two developmental points and these were designed to capture both morpho-syntactic and semantic development. The children's comprehension was also assessed. The measures of adult speech fell into four categories: length and formal complexity, non-verbal context, discourse features (for example, illocutionary force) and locus of reference. The last of these measures was concerned with the kind of activities that were referred to and the identity of participants. Adult speech was sampled at the start of the observation period.

The most striking finding to emerge from the Ellis and Wells analysis was that there were no differences in either the length or complexity of parental utterances addressed to the three groups of children. However, there were differences in the frequency with which parents used particular syntactic forms and engaged in particular conversational topics. The children who showed the earliest and most rapid language development—those in the EFD group—received significantly more acknowledgements, corrections, prohibitions and instructions from their parents than children in either of the other two groups. They also received more imitations, repetitions, directives and questions and heard more adult speech that referred to their own current activities and to current household activities. On all of these measures, children in the LFD group were intermediate between the EFS and SD groups, although the differences between the two less precocious groups were not significant.

The measures used by Ellis and Wells were all absolute frequencies rather than proportions, so one conclusion from their data is that *quantity* of adult speech appears to have an influence on language development. This is an aspect of their findings that has often been overlooked, perhaps because arguments about the sheer amount of language that children hear might be seen as behaviourist. However, it is significant to note that, in a recent study, Hoff-Ginsberg (1990) has also argued that the amount of speech used by mothers has a significant influence on language development.

Ellis and Wells (1980) also argue that particular qualitative aspects of adult speech are important for language development. They suggest that directives are helpful because parents of young children usually ask them to do something that relates to an object or action to which the child is already paying attention. Thus, most directives present the child with a linguistic encoding of something that the child has already encoded non-linguistically, and this is thought to make it easier for the child to acquire the word (or words) that the adult has used.

This explanation of the potential importance of directives for facilitating early language development runs counter to earlier claims that directive interactional styles may impede language development (Newport et al., 1977; Hoff-Ginsberg & Shatz, 1982). Indeed, Newport et al. go so far as to suggest that directives "rarely map clearly on to the non-linguistic context". However, as Ellis and Wells point out, this is not typically the case with the directives used to very young children and, as we will see in Chapter 5, adults tend to ask children to carry out actions that are closely related to their current activity.

Although Ellis and Wells do not do so, I think that it is possible to make a similar argument for the potentially facilitatory role of questions. As with directives, parents tend to ask young children questions about their immediate environment, since there is a reasonable chance that the child will be able to answer: parents ask about the identity and colour of objects rather than about the origins of the Universe. The same argument can also be extended to the case of the child's own activities and to current household activities—the two other categories of parental speech that were related to language development. Given that young children tend to be closely involved in the regular household activities like cleaning and washing up, it can be argued that references to these, as well as to the child's own activities, will provide the child with an opportunity to hear adult speech that refers to activities and objects to which he/she is already attending.

The Emergence of a Consensus

In one important sense, the data from the Bristol study can be seen as providing support for the arguments of Gleitman et al. (1984) that the effects of adult speech upon children's language development are strictly limited. Indeed, subsequent analysis of the data from the Bristol study (Barnes et al., 1983; Richards, 1990) has confirmed the specific finding of other studies that it is the development of auxiliaries that is most clearly related to adult speech; although it has become increasingly apparent that the relationship between child and adult use of auxiliaries is an extremely complex one.

From another perspective, however, the Bristol data can be seen as presenting a rather different picture from that offered by Gleitman et al. The arguments made by Ellis and Wells are, however, remarkably similar to those of Zukow, Reilly and Greenfield (1982). These authors concluded that a major shortcoming of studies investigating the relationship between adult speech and child language development was that they concentrated only on linguistic input and ignored the relationship between the language that the child hears and the non-verbal context in which that language occurs. A similar point was also made by Messer (1983) in his discussion of the relationship between maternal speech and concurrent non-verbal activity.

Careful reading of the literature of the early 1980s thus revealed that a consensus was beginning to emerge about the way in which children's language development and adult speech were related. This was that the influence of adult syntax upon children's language development was a very limited one. What appeared to be more important was the relationship between what adults said and the activity in which child and adult were engaged at the time of the utterance. As we will see in the next chapter, this view is one that has its theoretical roots in the work of Halliday and Bruner.

NOTES

1.   The MLU is calculated in morphemes rather than words. A morpheme is the smallest meaningful unit in a language. Thus a noun in its singular form is one morpheme, whereas the same noun in its plural form consists of two morphemes—the word stem and the plural morpheme, usually "s". A verb usually consists of two morphemes—the stem morpheme and the morpheme

marking tense. For example, "pushed" is made up of the stem morpheme "push" and the "ed" morpheme indicating past tense. At the outset of language development, each word is usually equivalent to a single morpheme because children take some time to learn about morphological endings.

2. Throughout this book I use the following convention for reporting ages—year: month. day. Thus 2:3 means 2 years 3 months old and 1:3.15 would mean 1 year 3 months 15 days old.

3. These were: MLU, verbs/utterance, noun phrases/utterance and auxiliaries/verb phrase.

CHAPTER THREE

The Social Context of Early Language Experience

The child has his or her own natural means for calling attention selectively to aspects of a scene. Interaction with an adult provides the child with an opportunity to learn the conventional or "non-natural" means for doing so.

Bruner (1983b)

Jerome Bruner has had a direct or indirect influence on much of the recent research into the relationship between language experience and early language development. In 1975, he published a seminal paper in which he argued that the young child does not encounter language as an isolated phenomenon but, rather, within the rich context provided by the social interaction that takes place between child and adult. This social interaction presents the child with a framework which provides vital support for the task of acquiring language. According to Bruner, the child is able to take account of the socio-interactional framework because the language that he/she hears typically provides a commentary upon, and interpretation of, the interaction in which the child is currently taking part. Thus, the close relationship between the social context and the language that the child hears, assists the child in "cracking the code" of language.

Later in this chapter I want to spell out Bruner's views—and some of their implications—in more detail. But first, it is relevant to note that

Bruner's arguments are firmly located in more general lines of research that emerged very strongly in the developmental psychology and linguistics of the late 1970s. The first of these was research into the social abilities of infants, which showed that children are born into the world as highly social beings endowed with a range of abilities that prepare them to develop complex patterns of interaction with the adults around them. The second significant trend in research was an increasing emphasis upon the pragmatic functions of language. In particular, the view of Michael Halliday (1975), which emphasised that children's early language serves social functions, attracted attention.

I have discussed the development of the first of these views in some detail elsewhere (Harris & Coltheart, 1986, ch. 5) and all I want to do here is to present a very brief overview of some of the seminal research into the social abilities of young infants (see also Schaffer, 1989a, 1989b, for recent reviews). I will then go on to discuss the work of Halliday.

THE SOCIAL ABILITIES OF INFANTS

For me, the most striking illustration of the inherently social nature of the infant initially came from the work of Trevarthen (1975), who carried out detailed analyses of video-recordings of young babies interacting with their mothers. Trevarthen found that babies of just a few weeks old behaved very differently depending upon whether they were interacting with another person or with an object. The infants' response to a moving object was to track it and often to reach out to it. The infants' response to people—and particularly to a familiar person such as the mother—was to smile and wave, and often to make marked lip movements.

Interestingly, a baby's special response to people only occurred when someone was actually paying attention. In one of Trevarthen's studies, mothers alternated between talking to their child and talking to another adult who was standing nearby. Although the mother always remained in the same position, immediately beside her baby, as soon as she turned her head away and began talking to the other adult, the baby stopped interacting with her and became much more passive.

The young infant's capacity for social interaction has a marked influence on the adults who are caring for the child. They respond to the baby's smiles and arm movements—and to crying and vocalisation—by engaging in interaction. Over the first few months of life, the patterns of interaction between adult and infant become more complex and routines—fixed patterns of interaction—develop. Such routines become particularly important during highly predictable parts of the infant's day such as feeding, nappy changing, bathtime and bedtime. But other routines develop during the increasingly long periods that the infant is awake and the caretakers are endeavouring to keep him/her amused. The routines described most frequently in the literature on early language development fall into this latter category and include such games as "peekaboo" and "give-and-take" (in which mother and child take it in turns to give and receive an object).

Much research has been devoted to charting the development of social routines. One significant finding is that there is a gradual change throughout the first year of life in the contribution that the infant is able to make to sustaining interaction. Even very young infants appear to have "conversations" with their mothers but, initially, this is because mothers tend to talk in the pauses that naturally occur in the infants' vocalising. Only later does the infant begin to vocalise in response to the mother (Schaffer, Collis & Parsons, 1977) and more genuine turn-taking appears.

A similar argument about the initial importance of the adult contribution to interaction has also been made in the case of visual attention. For example, Collis and Schaffer (1975) and Collis (1977) have shown that joint visual attention is common in the first year of life, i.e. mothers and babies tend to look at the same objects. They argue that, initially, joint attention arises because mothers tend to follow their children's line of regard but, in the second year of life, infants pay increasing attention to where their mother is looking. However, more recently, Butterworth (Butterworth & Grover, 1989; Butterworth & Jarrett, 1991) has shown that the looking behaviour of young infants is rather more sophisticated than the findings of Collis and Schaffer suggest. For example, babies as young as 6 months are successfully able to follow their mother's line of regard providing that the object of regard is in front of the infant and it is the first object that the baby encounters when turning to look. By 12 months, babies are still unable to locate a target that is behind them but they can locate a target even when it is not the first one that is encountered in turning to look. By 18 months, babies can successfully locate objects behind them although they are easily distracted if there is already something in their field of view.

Another important social development in infancy is that of pointing. Towards the end of the first year, infants show signs of understanding pointing. They look in the appropriate direction when someone else points (Leung & Rheingold, 1981; Schaffer, 1984). The ability to point appears to be uniquely human—even chimpanzees are incapable of using an outstretched arm and index finger to indicate—and right from its first appearance in infancy pointing appears to have an important communicative function. Babies begin to point at around 14 months and it seems clear that, even when it first emerges, pointing is used to direct attention. Infants typically check that their mothers are attending to the object of interest: they point and then turn to check that the mother is looking in the direction of the point. Butterworth and Franco (1990) found that pointing and checking were invariably accompanied by vocalisation, which supports the view that pointing is communicative. Interestingly, Butterworth and Franco also found that, by 15 months, infants would first check to see whether the mother was looking at them and only then point in order to redirect attention.

Being able to identify which object another person is looking at, and later being able to point out objects oneself, is very important for the development of social routines. Once a child understands the significance of pointing, for example, games involving objects (such as the adult asking the child "Where's the X?" or the child pointing at an object) form an important part of the developing communication between adult and child. However, parents are very good at exploiting the less sophisticated abilities of even tiny infants, and so social routines can begin to develop from the first weeks of the infant's life and gradually evolve as the infant becomes more competent.

By 6 months of age, many routines are well established and although, within a community, there may be a great commonality in the kind of routines that can be observed, each child and caretaker will have developed routines that are unique. Bower (1977) made the interesting suggestion that the uniqueness of routines explains, at least in part, why most infants suddenly become upset in the company of unfamiliar adults, at around the age of 7 months. Strangers do not act in predictable ways because they are unfamiliar with the routines that have developed around a particular child and young infants find this unpredictability stressful. If Bower is correct in his view, it strongly suggests that infants of this age have a very well-developed memory for familiar routines.

More recent research has suggested that infants are even able to violate the rules of familiar routines in order to engage in teasing. Reddy (1990, 1991) studied the development of interactional games between the ages of 7 months and 1 year. She claims that, even at this young age, infants perform incongruous acts in well-established routines to the mutual delight of infant and adult. In one such case, adult and child were taking part in a game of "give-and-take" in which the same object was handed back and forth. After several turns, the child handed the object to the adult and then, as the adult reached out to take it, snatched it back again.

Precisely what such observations imply for notions of infant humour may be arguable, but the fact that very young children are able to violate the rules of routines again suggests that they have a very well-developed ability to remember their structure.

Social interaction, then, forms a large part of the infant's experience throughout the first year of life. During this period, young children build up extensive knowledge of the pattern of frequently occurring social-interactional events in their lives and this provides an important context for learning. What of the language that the child first uses? Is this also, in some sense, social? According to Halliday (1975), it is.

A FUNCTIONAL–INTERACTIONAL ACCOUNT OF EARLY LANGUAGE DEVELOPMENT

As I mentioned at the beginning of this chapter, I see Halliday's conception of language as an important part of a more general view about the social origins of language in the child. Interestingly, it is clear that Bruner's own views were directly influenced by Halliday's writing, although this is not always apparent in some of his articles (see, for example, Bruner, 1983a, for explicit references to Halliday).

Halliday adopted what he describes as a "functional–interactional" approach to child language development. This approach differs from earlier accounts in two ways. First, it argues that language development should be viewed as one realisation of certain social functions such as instrumental ("I want"), regulatory ("do as I tell you") and interactional ("me and you"). For Halliday, early language development is to be interpreted as the child's progressive mastery of a functional potential and he claimed that, from the outset, children use language to influence the behaviour of others. This emphasis on the mastery of language function led directly to the second part of Halliday's thesis, which was that the child masters language functions in a social context:

> There is ... a further implication here, one which takes us into the social foundations of language. If, for example, language is used from an early stage to regulate the behaviour of others ... this assumes some general framework of social structure and social processes in terms of which a function such as "regulatory" makes sense. More particularly— since we are concerned with the language of the child—it presupposes a concept of cultural transmission. ... Here the concept of meaning, and of learning to mean, is in the last analysis interpreted in sociological terms, in the context of some chain of dependence such as: social order–transmission of that social order to the child–role of language in the transmission process–functions of language in relation to his role–meanings derived from these functions (Halliday, 1975, p.5).

For Halliday, then, language is a social phenomenon, both in terms of the functions that it initially serves for the child, and also because opportunities for the child to observe linguistic realisations of these functions occur within a social context. Interaction with adults provides the context in which a child can initially learn how these functions can be expressed through language.

One important component of Halliday's claim about the social-functional roots of language is that language functions are initially expressed by the child in non-conventional ways: Only later does the child learn how such functions are realised in the language that he/she hears and gradually adult forms replace the forms invented by the child. In other words, Halliday argues, there is a continuity in the functions but not the forms used in early child language.

My description of Halliday's account of language development may leave the reader wondering exactly how the general principles that I have described might operate in practice. This is a reaction that I have often experienced when reading Halliday because he often appears more concerned with the broad outline of his theory than with its detail. (This may be one reason why Halliday has had less influence on child language research than he might have done.) However, let me give you a flavour of the observation of his son, Nigel, that Halliday presents in *Learning how to mean*, in the hope that this will illuminate his theory.

When Nigel was 10½ months old, he used four different communicative functions: instrumental, regulatory, interactional and personal. All of these functions were expressed through the use of consistent forms, but these were all ones that Nigel had, in some sense, invented and they were not the same as adult forms. For example, there were two forms of the instrumental ("I want") function which were used when Nigel wanted something. One of these was a general request and the other was a specific request. Halliday glosses them as "give me that" and "give me my bird ". The first of these was expressed by the sound /na/ and the other by the sound /bo/ .

Over the next months, the number of specific demands that Nigel used increased to include (among others) a request for some powder, a Dvorak record to be played, and his potty. Expression of these demands remained idiosyncratic; Nigel was still not using any adult forms to express the various functions that he had acquired. By 16 months of age, however, Nigel began to use adult forms and the specific demands listed above were expressed through the use of the words "powder", "Dvorak" and "potty", respectively. General demands, however, continued to be expressed through non-adult forms—presumably because there is no single word that can be used for requests or demands.

One interesting consequence of Halliday's social-functional view of early language development is that it places the informative function of language in a much less central position:

The [informative] use of language in the sense of "I've got something to tell you", which tends to obsess adults, perhaps because they have learned it with so much difficulty, is irrelevant to a small child; it has no direct social meaning. It is also inaccessible to him, since it is wholly intrinsic to language; it is a function that derives from the nature of language itself. The other[s] ... are all extralinguistic: they arise, and can be realized independently of language (Halliday, 1975, p.64).

This is a view that is echoed in the writings of Bruner.

BRUNER'S THEORY

As one might expect with a theory originally formulated over 15 years ago, there have been some changes in the precise details of Bruner's argument. Since these changes are of some interest, I will begin by considering the original view (Bruner, 1975a, 1975b) and then discuss a more recent formulation (Bruner, 1983a, 1983b).

Bruner's original—and most important—insight was that children learn about language in the highly familiar context of social exchanges with caretakers. (Bruner, in fact, talks exclusively about mothers, but his arguments could apply to any adult who spends a great deal of time with a child.) According to Bruner, the familiar social context helps the child to interpret the language that occurs within it, since caretakers typically use language to interpret and comment upon the social context. (We will see some examples of the close relationship between language and context later in this chapter.) As Bruner expresses it, the child's knowledge of the social context—and especially of the routines that occur within it—assists the child to "crack the code" of the language that accompanies social interaction.

As with all important insights, Bruner's claim now seems self-evident. The only surprising thing is that it did not appear until the mid-1970s. However, if we remember the enormous influence that Chomsky had upon early research into child language, then it becomes clear why the focus of research in the late 1960s and early 1970s was upon the child's creative use of language and especially upon syntactic productivity (see, for example, Brown, 1973). Such a focus tends to obscure the fact that both the child's early experience and use of language take place in well-established social contexts.

I have just argued that Bruner's claim about the social context of early language development appears self-evident and it is certainly one that has had a significant influence upon my own research. However, I am less convinced by some of the detailed claims about the relationship between language development and social experience that Bruner made in 1975. For example, he claimed that children come to learn about the thematic roles of *agent* (the person who carries out an action) and *experiencer* (the person on the receiving end of an action) through the turn-taking games that they play with their mothers. Bruner also saw such games as important for learning about objects and their relationship to agents and experiencers. I see these claims as somewhat problematic for two reasons. First, they are firmly located within a particular linguistic theory, namely, Filmore's Case Grammar (Filmore, 1968). The thought is that children are actually learning about cases—such as *agent, object* and *experiencer*—and case relations—such as *agent–action, agent–experiencer, action–object*—as they begin to develop language. Secondly, Bruner places particular emphasis on certain kinds of routine—those that emerge from play—as providing necessary support for language development.

My worry about the first claim is that the suggestion that children acquire thematic roles from analysis of social interaction seems highly questionable. However, since Bruner himself dismissed this particular claim on a later occasion (Bruner, 1983b), it does not seem fair to continue to object to it. However, my worry about Bruner's emphasis on the importance of particular kinds of routine is a more serious one. Although play-based routines—or formats—such as "give-and-take" and "peekaboo" do have a role to play in early language development, I want to suggest that the notion of what constitutes a "routine" should be construed rather more widely than Bruner originally suggested. This is a point that I will return to when I discuss my findings concerning the relationship between language and social context in the speech addressed to young children. What I want to do now, however, is to discuss how Bruner modified his original view. A good place to read an account of the more recent version is Bruner (1983b).

It is a common move within psychology—as I suspect it is within other disciplines—to describe the original formulation of a view as a "strong" form and subsequently to advocate support for a "weaker" version of the same claim (see, for example, Cromer's, 1979, discussion of the two forms of the cognition hypothesis). Bruner (1983b) outlines two versions of the general claim that, if a child is aware of certain distinctions non-linguistically, learning them linguistically will be much easier. (Bruner actually uses the term "conceptually" rather than "non-linguistically", but I think this begs rather too many questions and, as far as I can see, the use of the more neutral term in no way changes the argument.)

The strong version of this claim is that there is some kind of isomorphism between language and the world. Thus, a child will acquire certain concepts through interaction with the world and these are the same concepts that are realised in language. Language is the way that it is because of the way that the world is, and learning about the world will thus allow the child to acquire language.

Bruner gives some nice examples of how this isomorphism between language and the world might operate:

> ... one might claim that the universal linguistic distinction, MARKED–UNMARKED, exists in all languages by virtue of its conformance [sic] to something intrinsic in human attention, or that case grammar is easily grasped because we already know in some non-linguistic way about the arguments of action and that the grammar is some sort of "distillation" of non-linguistic knowledge (Bruner, 1983b, p.27).

Notice that these are claims about the acquisition of grammatical distinctions. According to the strong hypothesis, the rules of social interaction are the same as rules of grammar.

As Bruner says, this is a seductive argument, and the reference to case grammar in the previous quotation will have alerted the reader to the fact that this strong hypothesis was the one that Bruner himself was advocating in 1975. His preferred view in 1983 was somewhat different:

> I have come to the conclusion that systems of language—and I emphasize the systematicity of language here—are autonomous problem spaces that, however much their conquest may be aided by non-linguistic knowledge or external support from others, must be mastered on their own (Bruner, 1983b, p.28).

One of the main arguments that Bruner puts forward as a reason for having moved away from a strong claim about the isomorphism of language and the world is particularly interesting. This claim is that "well-formedness in language" is determined by rules that are solely language-internal and do not have any non-linguistic counterpart. In making this claim, it would appear that Bruner was thinking in particular of morpho-syntactic rules. But, in fact, a great deal of language does not involve any simple word–world mapping. For example, deictic terms like *you*, *me*, *this* and *that* pose children difficulties precisely because they have a context-dependent relationship to the world, and superordinate terms are also problematic because their use involves understanding that an object in the world can be described in more than one way.

I think that these concerns about the extent to which language and the world are isomorphic are important and they encapsulate a general feeling among many child language researchers that too much emphasis has been placed on the idea that a child can exploit the redundancy between adult speech and an observable world when developing language. This point has been made particularly clearly—and for a considerable time—by Karmiloff-Smith (see, for example, Karmiloff-Smith, 1979; Cuckle & Karmiloff-Smith, 1988) in her discussion of language as a special problem-space for children.

Perhaps more tellingly for the present discussion, a somewhat different worry about the extent to which language relates to children's experience of the world has been made by researchers such as Messer (1983) and Collis (1985), who have been concerned with non-verbal precursors of early language development. Like Bruner, they have questioned the extent to which there is a simple continuity between pre-linguistic and linguistic behaviour, even in cases where there is considerable similarity between the two (see, for example, the discussion of pre-linguistic and linguistic turn-taking by Collis, 1985).

Where does that leave Bruner? The answer is that he sees a weaker version of his original claim as still tenable. The weaker version goes something like this: The child's experience of social interaction will lead him/her to discover what it is that language is designed to distinguish in the real world; when the child hears language being uttered in the presence of distinctions that have already been distinguished non-linguistically, this will alert him/her to relevant linguistic distinctions. Bruner is quite clear about why this is a much weaker claim than the one he made earlier:

> It is a weak claim in the sense that it has nothing to say about the naturalness of certain grammatical forms, *indeed nothing to say about grammatical forms altogether*. Its claim is only that it is immeasurably valuable, in learning a code, to know already what the code "stands for" (Bruner, 1983b, p.29; emphasis added).

It has always seemed to me that Bruner's original arguments about the "naturalness" of language were something of a red herring and not necessary to the rest of his claims. So, for me, what is most notable about Bruner's characterisation of his revised view is the move away from arguments about grammatical form. What he emphasises in his 1983 chapter (Bruner, 1983b) is that the social context in which the young child encounters language paves the way for learning about communicative intent. Initially, the child discovers non-linguistic ways to express such intentions: Later, the child masters appropriate linguistic ways for the realisation of such intentions. In this formulation, developing language is seen as the acquisition of pragmatic categories.

You may find that this argument about the relationship between language and the social context is a familiar one. The reason for this sense of *déjà vu* is that Bruner's argument is very similar to that made by Halliday. Halliday talks about the continuity between the pre-linguistic and linguistic expression of functions, whereas Bruner talks about a continuity in the expression of pragmatic distinctions. But the essence of their argument is the same: The social context of language experience provides the young child with an important opportunity to learn about certain communicative functions which are initially expressed by the child in pre-linguistic ways; the early stage of learning how to use language consists of learning how to express these functions in a linguistic form.

Bruner devotes a considerable time to considering specific examples of how this general principle might operate in practice. However, rather than discussing these examples, I want to turn to a discussion of my own research in this area.

THE NON-VERBAL CONTEXT OF EARLY LANGUAGE EXPERIENCE

Both Bruner and Halliday had an important influence on my initial thinking about the relationship between early language development and early social interaction. I was convinced that the outline of their argument was correct. What I was less sure about was its detail: What precisely were the aspects of early language development that might be intimately related to children's early social experiences?

In the previous chapter, I highlighted the generally negative results that emerged from studies of the relationship between the rate at which a child develops language and aspects of the adult speech to which the child is exposed. I argued that one reason why such studies might have failed to find a relationship between language development and language experience was that they were exclusively concerned with linguistic input, while ignoring the wider context in which that linguistic input occurred. The work of Bruner and Halliday strongly suggests that the wider social context of children's linguistic experience is a more appropriate domain for study, and that, before one can conclude that language development is *not* related to language experience, it is first necessary to examine both the language addressed to young children and the social context in which children encountered that language.

As we saw in Chapter 2, the potential significance of the non-verbal context of adult speech was also highlighted by empirical studies of adult speech to children, notably the Bristol study. However, the Bristol study did not set out to present a detailed description of the relationship between adult speech and its non-verbal context and the starting point for my own research was the desire to answer a very specific but basic question about the social-interactional context of early language experience. It was this: What *is* the precise relationship between the non-verbal and verbal aspects of children's early social experience? In other words, what do parents talk about to their children, and how does what they say relate to the concurrent non-verbal context?

CHAPTER FOUR

From Input to Uptake: Traversing a Methodological Minefield

In this chapter I want to underline some of the major theoretical and methodological difficulties that arise in attempting to consider the extent to which language development is influenced by children's exposure to adult speech. The essence of the problem is to decide, first, what kind of evidence has a bearing on this issue and, secondly, how appropriate evidence can best be collected.

WHAT KIND OF EVIDENCE?

As we saw in Chapter 2, the most common approach has been to look for correlations between measures of adult speech and measures of child language development in an attempt to draw conclusions about the influence of the former upon the latter. This approach gives rise to all sorts of potential problems, not least that patterns of cause-and-effect are notoriously difficult to disentangle in a correlational design.

The problems of the interdependence of child and adult speech have commonly been addressed by taking measures of adult language at t_1 and then relating these to measures of child language development over subsequent months. This design avoids many of the problems of interpretation that arise when both child and adult speech are sampled at the same time. For, given that mothers are sensitive to the language level of their own child, they will adjust their own speech to a level that they deem appropriate. Thus a child with advanced language is likely to have a mother whose language is more complex than that used by the mother of a child with less advanced language. A relationship between child and maternal speech sampled at the same time will thus reveal nothing about whether the child's own level of language development has been causally influenced by the mother's speech.

Investigating the relationship between maternal speech and subsequent child language development does not, however, solve all the problems. One potential problem has been highlighted in a recent paper by Yoder and Kaiser (1989). They draw attention to the difficulty of distinguishing between direct and indirect patterns of influence from mother to child. Returning to the example of auxiliary development discussed in Chapter 2, a direct influence would be one in which the child's own use of auxiliaries is related to maternal use of auxiliaries. An indirect influence would be one which is brought about through the influence of another variable that co-varies with auxiliary use. For example, Hoff-Ginsberg (1987) found that mothers most often used auxiliaries in their speech when they were requesting unknown information. She also showed that such requests were associated with faster language development. Requests for information in general have also been shown to be associated with faster language development when the child's response to the request is followed up with an extended comment (Howe, 1980). Increasing use of auxiliaries is an important component of developing language competence. Thus, it could be that the child's greater use of auxiliaries comes about through being given opportunities to provide information rather than to hear auxiliaries being used.

In large samples, the existence of co-varying variables can be examined statistically by looking at the intercorrelation of child language at t_1, maternal speech at t_1 and later child language development (Yoder & Kaiser, 1989). However, this is not an option where only a small number of children are studied.

Yoder and Kaiser also discuss influences that children exert upon their mothers' language. Children's language ability has a very powerful influence on the way that adults talk. Adults adjust—fine-tune—their speech as their children's linguistic competence grows. More particularly, as Cross et al. (1980) showed, when adults talk to children they are particularly sensitive to the child's own level of comprehension.

There have been two main ways of assessing children's language development, both involving comparisons between child language at t_1 and at t_2. In one design, a sample of children is selected such that age and language ability at the first observation (t_1) are equated. In the second design, the competence of the children is equated statistically by partialling out both age and language ability at the first observation. In both cases, the matching of initial level of language development—development at t_1—is done on the basis of the child's level of language production. As the reader will no doubt have spotted, one potential problem with both approaches is that, even if children are equated for level of language production, they may still have differing levels of comprehension, and this could lead to differences both in adult speech and in the rate of subsequent language development.

One approach might be to assess children's comprehension as well as production at the start of a study. However, obtaining a reliable measure of the language comprehension of a child in the early stages of development is extremely difficult and, fortunately, there is some evidence that adult speech has a rather weaker relationship to children's comprehension than might be supposed. This evidence comes from the paper by Ellis and Wells (1980), where data are reported on comprehension as well as production (see Chapter 2). What Ellis and Wells found was that:

> ... where there was a significant association between a variable in adult speech and increase in the children's linguistic maturity, the strongest association tended to be with indices derived from spontaneous speech production. ... Correlations with child comprehension were in all cases smaller and often not statistically significant (Ellis & Wells, 1980, p.53).

This finding suggests that, providing children are equated for initial level of language production, it is possible to draw conclusions about relationships between language development and adult speech.

Questions arise, however, both about the selection of an appropriate time period over which to assess language development and over the choice of developmental measures. The essence of the problem is that language development involves the development of many different abilities which are of varying importance at particular ages and stages. It is unlikely that the same features of adult speech will be related to each of these various components of language development. Indeed, the evidence reviewed in Chapter 2 suggests that relationships between adult speech and language development are extremely specific. Thus what is needed are studies that consider particular aspects of development over relatively short periods of time, and which select aspects of development and measures of adult speech about which it is possible to make theoretical claims. It is essential to be able to explain why a particular measure of adult speech might be related to a particular feature of child language development, since this will provide a clear theoretical base from which to develop appropriate methodology.

FROM INPUT TO UPTAKE

Being able to give a theoretical account of the relationship between aspects of adult speech and child language development gets over another problem, namely distinguishing between language input and language uptake. Language input is adult speech, but language uptake is that part of the input that is actually attended to by the child. What is important here is the notion that children selectively attend to the adult speech directed to them. They pay most attention to those utterances—or parts of an utterance—that are interpretable or nearly interpretable at their current level of ability. The distinction between input and uptake is important because it forces us to attempt to take the child's view of adult language and to consider whether adult-centred descriptions of input are actually a reflection of language uptake. For it is language uptake, rather than language input, that is most relevant to our understanding of a child's language experience and its relationship to language development.

Another important theoretical consideration concerns the kind of relationship that might exist between language development and adult speech. As we saw in Chapter 2, the debate is not about whether the two are related in some way but about the extent to which language experience is essential (although not, of course, sufficient) for language development. There are various possibilities. One is that language development will never occur unless adult speech contains certain kinds of feature. This is a very strong claim, although, in one sense, it is not a controversial one as we saw in Chapter 1: Even strongly nativist accounts recognise the need for some linguistic data; and cases of extreme linguistic deprivation (such as Genie, described in Curtiss, 1977) bear witness to the fact that children do not develop language if no one talks to them. However, this is not the position that I am attempting to defend in this book. As I noted earlier, my argument has to do with notions of relative frequency and relative delay and it is this: If certain crucial features occur infrequently in adult speech, language development is likely be delayed.

Note that it does not follow from this argument that a superfluity of the right kind of features will inevitably lead to very rapid language development. It is theoretically possible that, if linguistic input facilitates development, then the "better" the input the faster the child's development. But I think that this is unlikely to be the case. It seems to me that there are quite tight constraints on the maximum amount of influence that input can have upon development. So what I am proposing is a kind of threshold model in which what matters is that there be a sufficiency of the right kind of experience. If the child receives linguistic input that does not provide such a sufficiency, then early language development will be affected. But if this sufficiency is greatly exceeded, there will be little or no additional facilitatory effect.

A final point to make is that my argument concerns the significance of linguistic input *given that all else is equal*. Strictly, what I am proposing is that, in cases of significantly non-optimal input, children's language progress will be delayed in comparison to the rate of progress that would have occurred *had the input been different*. Obviously, this claim cannot be tested directly because it is impossible to observe what progress might have been like. However, if one compares two groups of children of *roughly similar ability*, who differ only in the kind of linguistic input that they receive, then there should be differences among the children in terms of their early linguistic progress.

Note the point about "roughly similar ability". Some children do have serious difficulties in acquiring language that are not in any way environmentally determined. For some children, slow language development is only one aspect of a general learning difficulty. For others—specifically language-impaired children—language development seems to present a particular problem. In both cases, the difficulty arises from some kind of processing limitation and not from limitations of language experience.

Having considered what kind of evidence is relevant to arguments about the relationship between language experience and early language development, I will now turn to methodological questions concerning the collection of data.

OBTAINING APPROPRIATE EVIDENCE

There are essentially two different approaches to the study of early child language. The first involves the selection of a relatively large sample of children from whom data are collected at periodic intervals. The second concentrates on a much smaller sample but collects a relatively larger amount of data from each child. It is this latter approach that I adopted in all of the studies that I describe in this book. Furthermore, I think that it is the only approach that can yield data of sufficient detail to investigate the complex relationship between language and context.

In common with the majority of studies in this area, I chose to look at the linguistic experience that children obtain from their mothers. This does not mean that I consider mothers to be uniquely important as providers of linguistic experience. Fathers have an important role too (see Lewis & Gregory, 1987). However, in the case of the children that I have studied, their mothers certainly spent the greatest amount of time with them. This was because, with the exception of my study of deaf children, I have always studied first-born children whose mothers stayed at home with them full-time for at least the first 12 months.

The main reason for restricting my research to first-born children was to reduce one potentially important source of variability in language experience: There is good evidence that children with older siblings have a rather different kind of linguistic experience from first-borns (see Woollett, 1986). The children in my studies were also similar to one another in that they came from middle-class homes.

The decision to prefer homogeneity to heterogeneity was a methodological one. When I started this research I had relatively little idea about what I would discover about maternal speech and, in particular, I was unclear about how much inter-subject variation there would be. For this reason, it seemed important to reduce the inherent variability of the sample as much as possible.

Another methodological decision concerned the method of observation. In view of the need to collect detailed information not only about maternal speech but also its non-verbal context, it was decided to videotape all observation sessions. Mothers brought their children to the psychology department at Birkbeck College every 2 months where they were filmed through a one-way mirror in a recording studio. A 20-min video-recording was made at each session as well as an independent audio-recording.

The room in which the mothers and children were filmed was designed to be comfortable and relaxing. It was approximately 5 x 3 m—about the size of a small living room—and there were pictures on the walls, floor cushions, carpet and curtains. There were also two chairs, on one of which a large teddy bear was seated, and a toy box containing a selection of toys and books. The mothers were asked to imagine that they were at home and had some time to spend with their child. They were deliberately not given more specific instructions (even when they asked). All they were told was that we were interested in children's development, and particularly with the development of play and language. The mothers were not told—nor did they guess—that their own language would be analysed.

The reader may wonder whether the filming of mother and child though a one-way mirror in a psychology department laboratory can reveal anything about normal interaction. However, as a result of having carried out this study, I am convinced that, in the right circumstances, it can. One important consideration was that all the studies described in the following chapters were longitudinal and visiting the laboratory became a familiar experience for both the children and their mothers. One or two of the mothers were initially self-conscious about being filmed but any anxieties disappeared after their first visit. Another factor was that what occurred during the observation sessions was greatly influenced by the children's behaviour. And the children were far too young to appreciate that they were being filmed. For them, the laboratory was an exciting place where they came to play and they were completely oblivious to the presence of the microphones and the cameras behind the one-way mirror.

Using a laboratory setting, rather than filming in the child's home, gave us the enormous advantage of being able to use three cameras (two in the studio and one filming through the one-way mirror) and a mixer to provide comprehensive coverage of the activity in which mother and child were engaged. This proved to be invaluable for establishing the precise non-verbal context of individual maternal utterances.

CHAPTER FIVE

What Adults Say to Children

STUDY 1:
THE NON-VERBAL CONTEXT OF SPEECH TO
YOUNG CHILDREN

My research into the non-verbal context of parental speech fell into two stages. The initial aim was to discover what the relationship was between the language that young children hear and the social context in which that language occurs and, with this aim in mind, I began a small longitudinal study in 1981 with my colleague, David Jones.

The study grew and in the end we observed nearly 30 children. This provided us with an unexpected opportunity to study a small group of children with relatively slow language development as well as observing normal language development. But this came later, and it is described in the second part of this chapter. I begin by describing the original study, more formal accounts of which can be found in Harris, Jones and Grant (1983, 1984/5).

Analysis of the Interaction

As I mentioned in the previous chapter, data for this study came from 20-min video-recordings made every 2 months in our laboratory. Three recordings were selected for analysis from each of eight mother–child dyads. The first two recordings were made when the children were 7 and 9 months of age and in the final session the children were 16 months old.

The first stage in analysing the relationship between maternal speech and non-verbal aspects of the interaction was to produce a detailed transcript of 10 continuous minutes of the video-recording. The 10-min period began when mother and child had settled down and had become accustomed to the laboratory.

The transcript described everything that the mother and child did and said. Particular attention was paid to the order in which verbal and non-verbal events occurred; events that occurred at the same time were placed side by side on the same line of the transcript. An example of the transcription format is shown in Table 5.1.

The first analysis that was carried out on the transcriptions was an episode analysis of maternal speech. This was very similar to an analysis carried out by David Messer (1978, 1980) and it divides a mother's speech into episodes, where an episode consists of a series of utterances about the same topic.

Dividing maternal speech into episodes is not as easy a task as it might first appear, because there are various possible ways in which a "new topic" could be defined. From an adult perspective, most of the speech produced by the mothers in our sample might be considered to concern only one topic, the immediate social context. However, from the theoretical perspective of early language development, it is necessary to make quite fine-grained distinctions. Accordingly, on every occasion that a mother stopped talking about one object, such as a toy, and started talking about a different object, such as another toy, this was counted as being the start of a new episode. However, it was not always the case that the start of a new episode involved reference to a new object. Reference to a different activity involving the same object also counted as a new episode. For example, if a mother was talking about building the bricks into a tower and then began talking about the different colours of the bricks, this counted as a change in topic. Cases where the mother turned from talking about an object or activity to commenting on the child's internal state (such as hunger, thirst or other discomfort) were also counted as new episodes. Table 5.2 shows how the extract shown in Table 5.1 was divided into verbal episodes. Some of the episodes begin with the reference to a new object; others begin with reference to a new activity.

One important methodological consideration in identifying a new episode in maternal speech was that the division into episodes was made solely on the basis of what the mother said. No account was taken of the non-verbal behaviour of either the mother or the child, nor of the child's vocalisations. This was essential to the methodology, because the next

TABLE 5.1
Example of Transcription Format:
Mother and Child are Both Sitting on the Floor at the Start of this Extract
Next to a Toy Box. The Child is Playing with a Toy Train

Time	Mother	Child (age 16 months)
06:24	puts finger inside wagon of toy train **You can put things in there.** **What do you want to put in there?**	
		vocalises
	placing wagon closer to C **What are you going to put in there?** **Hey?**	
06:27		linking up wagons of toy train
	Join them up **What are you going to put in there?** looks in toy box	pushes wagons along floor
06:31	rummaging in toy box **Some bricks?**	
		vocalises, points at M
	takes teddy from toy box showing teddy to C **How about him?**	takes teddy from M and puts in wagon picks up teddy and shows to M
	leans across to look at teddy	
06:42	**That's a teddy isn't it, look?**	
		vocalises, holds teddy out to M
	points at teddy's eye **Yes, there's his eye.** points at teddy's other eye **There's his other eye** holds teddy out to C	
		takes hold of teddy's legs
06:57	**There's his toes.**	

Key: Vocalisations in **bold**; non-verbal activity in normal font. C = child; M = mother.

stage in the analysis was to take the start of each verbal episode and then check back through the transcript to determine what—if anything—had prompted the start of the episode. Cases where a new episode began in response to something said or done by the child were classed as *child-initiated*; cases where a new episode was not related to any activity of the child's were classed as *mother-initiated*.

TABLE 5.2
Episode Structure of Extract Shown in Table 5.1

Episode	Mother	Child (age 16 months)
1. Mother-initiated	puts finger inside wagon of toy train **You can put things in there.** . . . . **Hey?**	
2. Child-initiated	**Join them up**	linking up wagons of toy train
3. Mother-initiated	**What are you going to put in there?** looks in toy box	
4. Mother-initiated	takes teddy from toy box showing teddy to C **How about him?**	
5. Child-initiated	**That's a teddy isn't it, look?**	picks up teddy and shows to M
6. Child-initiated	points at teddy's eye **Yes, there's his eye.**	**vocalises**, holds teddy out to M
7. Child-initiated	**There's his toes.**	takes hold of teddy's legs

Child-initiated episodes were then subdivided according to the kind of event to which the mother had responded in starting a new verbal episode. There were three different kinds of event: a change in the child's direction of gaze, an action of the child's or a child vocalisation. Mother-initiated episodes were subdivided according to the way in which the mother introduced the new episode: A distinction was made between initiations that were purely verbal and those that were accompanied either by a relevant change in maternal gaze or by a relevant maternal action. Some examples of different kinds of episode are shown in Table 5.3.

Having determined the episode structure of an interaction, a second analysis was carried out on individual maternal utterances. All utterances were coded according to their immediate non-verbal context. This involved the use of an important distinction between utterances that had a context that was current and those that did not. An utterance was counted as having a *current* context only if it referred to an action, object or event on which the child was focusing attention at the time of the utterance. All other cases of reference were counted as having a *potential* context.

TABLE 5.3
Examples of Different Kinds of Episode

Initiator	Initiating Event	Accompanying Maternal Activity	Example
Mother	none	action	M puts finger inside toy wagon M: **You can put things in there.**
Child	gaze	gaze	C looks up at picture on wall M turns to look at same picture M: **That's a bee.**
Child	action	none	C picks up toy telephone and holds receiver to ear M: **Say "hello".**
Child	action + vocalisation	action	C vocalises and points at picture in book M points at same picture M: **Ball.**

Key: M = mother; C = child.

A potential context occurred when an utterance did not refer to anything on which the child was focusing attention at the time. In most cases, such references were to objects that were present in the room or to activities in which both mother and child were engaged at some time during the recording session. The crucial point, however, was that the child was not actually attending to these objects or engaging in these actions at the time that the utterance occurred.

In addition to reference to objects and activities, there were also some utterances that referred to the child's internal state. These were coded as having either a current context, if they described the child's internal state at the time of the utterance, or a potential context, if they referred to a non-current state. Some examples of utterance coding are shown in Table 5.4. It will be seen that utterances were typically coded as having more than one context, for example, a current object and a potential action. It will also be seen that references to the actions of the mother were distinguished from references to those of the child, and references to attributes of objects (such as colour or size) were also coded.

Results

One of the most striking findings to emerge from this study was that, across the age range that we considered, the proportion of episodes in which the mother responded to an initiation by the child remained remarkably constant at about two-thirds. On the other third of

TABLE 5.4
Examples of Maternal Utterance Coding

	Mother's Action		Child's Action		Object		Attribute		Child's Internal State	
	Cur.	Pot.	Cur.	Pot.	Cur.	Pot.	Cur.	Pot.	Cur.	Pot.
C picks up two bricks **You're picking up two again**			x		x					
M is making a tower with bricks **Look, I'm building up something for you**	x				x					
M and C look at reflections in mirror **Shall we go over to the mirror?**		x		x	x					
C holding teddy bear **He's such a big bear**					x		x			
C looking at teddy **But your little teddy is orange and this one is a lemon teddy**					x	x	x	x		
C protests as M shows him cube **You don't like that cube do you?**					x				x	

Key: Cur. = current reference; Pot. = potential reference.
Mothers' utterances are shown in **bold**.

occasions, mothers spontaneously initiated new verbal episodes. Table 5.5 shows the mean proportions of mother- and child-initiated episodes at 7, 9 and 16 months.

At first sight, the data in Table 5.5 may not appear particularly striking, since they suggest that mothers carried on behaving in the same way from 6 to 16 months. But, it is important to consider how much the children changed in the period of observation. At the start of the study, they were only just capable of sitting up and their ability to play with objects was severely limited by their level of motor development; but by 16 months, all of the children were walking and they were capable

TABLE 5.5
Mean Proportions of Mother-initiated and Child-initiated Episodes

	Type of Episode	
Age of Child	Mother-initiated	Child-initiated
7 months	0.34	0.66
10 months	0.31	0.69
16 months	0.28	0.72

of engaging in a range of sophisticated motor activities. This suggests that the highly stable ratio of mother- to child-initiations arose because mothers adapted their behaviour as their children's competence increased.

The way that mothers adjust their responses is illustrated by the data in Table 5.6, which shows the proportions of different kinds of initiations in episodes where the mother responded to a change in the child's activity. Here it can be seen that, at 7 months, mothers most frequently began a new episode in response to a change in the child's direction of gaze. At this age, the remaining episodes—just over 40%—began in response to a change in the child's activity. By 9 months, the picture had changed; only a tiny proportion of child-initiated episodes were triggered by a change in the child's gaze and over 80% were stimulated by an action of the child's. Action continued to be an important component in initiation and, at 16 months, over 80% of child-initiated episodes involved action. However, half of these initiations also involved a vocalisation. In other words, at 16 months, mothers frequently began a new episode in response to the child performing an action and simultaneously vocalising. (As I will show later, the children in this sample did not have any reliable words at 16 months, and so the mothers relied on the child's accompanying action in order to make a plausible interpretation of what the child was attempting to say.)

TABLE 5.6
Mean Proportions of Different Types of Initiation in Child-initiated Episodes

	Type of Initiation				
Age of Child	Vocalisation	Gaze	Voc. + Gaze	Action	Voc. + Action
7 months	0.00	**0.57**	0.00	0.43	0.00
10 months	0.00	0.14	0.03	**0.72**	0.11
16 months	0.05	0.07	0.01	**0.43**	**0.44**

Key: Most frequent category (or categories) at each age is shown in **bold**.

There was also another change from 9 to 16 months in mothers' responses to child-initiations. At the earlier sessions, the mothers usually accompanied their utterance with an action even though their own utterance had been prompted by the child's action. So, at 9 months, a typical child-initiated episode would begin with the mother commenting on something her child was doing while simultaneously providing an action of her own that acted as an additional cue to what she was saying. However, by 16 months, the mothers were much less likely to provide such additional non-verbal cues and 50% of the initial utterances in child-initiated episodes were not accompanied by maternal action. Presumably, this was because the mothers placed more reliance on the children's developing comprehension but, even so, since the majority of child-initiated episodes had an action context set up by the child, there was still a very close tying of episodes to actions.

Before turning to mother-initiated episodes, I want to underline what I see as the centrality of the child's action as a stimulus to the initiation of new verbal episodes. In this context, it should be noted that several authors have drawn attention to the significance of gaze as a cue to joint reference (see, for example, Bruner, 1975b; Collis, 1977; Schaffer, 1975; Messer, 1983). In one study, described in the previous chapter, Collis and Schaffer (1975) observed mother–infant dyads in a room which was bare except for a number of brightly coloured toys. They found that the mothers and infants tended to look at the same objects. (As I mentioned earlier, this was initially because the mothers followed the direction of their children's looking but later joint visual attention became more reciprocal.)

Carefully controlled laboratory conditions may not, however, provide the best model of joint attention in the real world. Although joint visual attention may provide an unambiguous cue in the visually uncluttered environment of a laboratory, it is much less likely to do so in the home— except in special circumstances such as book reading. At the end of a typical day spent in the company of an active 1-year-old, most caretakers have to tidy up the room (or rooms) in which the child has been playing. And in our laboratory, as at home, the first thing that the children did was to upend the toy box and tip all of the toys onto a heap on the floor. In such a situation, it is relatively difficult to be certain about exactly what another person—be it child or mother—is looking at.

In contrast to gaze, action provides a much less ambiguous cue as to the focus of another person's attention. Once a child has touched or picked up an object, the mother can assume with a fair degree of confidence that that toy is the object of the child's attention; and I think that is one of this reasons why mothers so often used the child's action as a stimulus for the start of a new episode.

TABLE 5.7
Mean Proportions of Different Types of Initiation in Mother-initiated Episodes

| | | Type of Initiation | |
Age of Child	Verbal	Verbal + Gaze	Verbal + Action
7–10 months	0.02	0.00	0.98
16 months	0.02	0.03	0.95

Action also played an important part in mother-initiated episodes. As Table 5.7 shows, regardless of the age of the child, the mothers almost invariably initiated an episode by accompanying their opening utterance with an action that served to cue the child. (The data from the 7- and 10-month sessions have been pooled as they were so similar.) Thus, from 10 months onwards, the great majority of new episodes began with the mother commenting upon an action. In the case of child-initiated episodes, it was a comment on the child's action; in the case of mother-initiated episodes, it was a comment upon her own action.

The close relationship between maternal speech and concurrent activity was also apparent in the analysis of individual maternal utterances. Table 5.8 shows the proportions of utterances with current and potential referents. (For simplicity, the data from the 7- and 9-month observations have been conflated since they were very similar.) The most important point to note is that the great majority of maternal utterances referred to an object that was at the child's current focus of attention. Relatively few utterances had potential contexts and, with one important exception, the proportions of current references in each category exceeded the proportions of potential references. The significant exception was child action where, at both ages, there were more references to potential child actions than to current child actions.

TABLE 5.8
Mean Proportions of Current and Potential References in Mothers' Utterances

| | Age of Child | | | |
| | 7–10 months | | 16 months | |
Reference	Current	Potential	Current	Potential
Mother's action	0.03	0.03	0.03	0.02
Child's action	0.09	0.19	0.10	0.23
Object	0.67	0.04	0.78	0.05
Attribute	0.38	0.05	0.32	0.06
Child's internal state	0.11	0.00	0.03	0.00

(References to maternal actions were so infrequent that a similar comparison was not possible.)

The explanation for mothers' frequent references to potential actions but current objects lies in the arguments that I set out earlier in this chapter. There, I endorsed Bruner's claim that early language development takes place in the context of highly familiar—and predictable—social routines. Within this highly predictable context, it is possible for the mother to comment on future action that will shortly be carried out with objects on which the child is focusing attention. For example, one situation that commonly occurred was for the mother to build up a tower of bricks as the child watched with mounting excitement. Then she would ask the child, "Are you going to knock it down?", and invariably the child did so. The point here is not that the child necessarily understood what the mother was saying, but that the action she was describing was entirely predictable from the context. Thus, although the action was a potential one in the physical sense, it is plausible to assume that it was in the mind of the child at the time of the utterance.

If a large number of references to potential actions are classed as "current" for the reason I have just outlined, then it is even more striking to consider how many utterances have a current context of some kind.

Maternal Speech and Children's Language Development

At the start of this study, it seemed likely that there would be close tying of maternal speech to the non-verbal context; what could not have been predicted was how close the relationship would be. The clearest indication of the closeness of language and context is that, at 16 months, nearly 80% of mothers' utterances referred to an object on which the child was focusing attention *at the time of the utterance*.

This finding is consistent with data reported by Masur (1982) on the verbal labels that mothers supply to children's early pointing gestures; and it also supports the finding of an earlier study by Messer (1978, 1980) that between 73 and 96% of mothers' references to toys were made at the same time that that toy was being manipulated.

If you think about this for a moment—and particularly if you have had experience of interacting with children under the age of 18 months—you will realise what a feat it is to be able to relate so much of what you say to the immediate focus of a small child's attention. It requires very close monitoring of what the child is doing and, in particular, it requires that you enter into the child's world and join in, and comment upon, joint activity.

Knowing how to talk to a small child does not come easily to everyone, and it requires considerable energy to monitor a child's activity and then join in at exactly the right moment. So one question that arose immediately from the results of this study was whether all mothers would show the pattern of close relationship between their language and the immediate non-verbal context that was evident in our small sample. If there was variation among mothers—as seemed likely—then there was another question of interest to be asked: Does it make a difference to the child if the language that he/she hears is not closely related to the immediate non-verbal context?

Before I turn to some data that are relevant to this question, I think it is important to consider why it might be important for early language development that the child hears language that is very closely related to the immediate non-verbal context. As I will argue in the next chapter, I think that it is possible to give a very specific answer to this question when one considers early lexical development. However, for the moment, I want to couch the argument in rather general terms because, unless I do so, it will be difficult to explain the more specific argument.

The general idea is a fairly simple one and it owes its origin to the work of Wells and his co-workers (Ellis & Wells, 1980; Barnes et al., 1983), which I discussed in Chapter 2. Wells argues that early language development is facilitated if the speech that the child hears refers to objects with which the child is directly involved at the time of speaking. This is because such language experience will encode events to which the child is already attending and which he/she will have encoded enactively or iconically (to use the terminology of Bruner, Olver & Greenfield, 1966). In other words, the child learns to encode linguistically by hearing language associated with previously non-symbolic encodings.

There are, of course, several problems with this argument. Not the least of these is that it begs the question of which of the many possible pairings of language with a previously encoded event will be selected by the child. The child will hear a huge number of such pairings, but it is very unlikely that they will all be treated with equal significance. Apart from anything else, processing limitations would require severe selection from the linguistic data that are potentially available.

This is a problem that I will return to at the end of this chapter but, for the purposes of considering the next study, it is necessary only to entertain the hypothesis that language development would be facilitated if language input consists of a high proportion of utterances that refer to actions and objects on which the child is currently focusing attention.

STUDY 2:
THE NON-VERBAL CONTEXT OF MATERNAL
SPEECH AND RATE OF LANGUAGE
DEVELOPMENT

The second study of maternal speech came about largely by accident. Once word got out that researchers at Birkbeck College were interested in filming mothers and babies, we were inundated with offers from people who wanted to take part in the study. It seemed a good idea to film as many mother–baby pairs as possible and so we carried on adding to our sample until new projects left us with no more time for filming.

Initial analysis concentrated on the first eight mother–baby pairs who were able to stay with the project until the children reached the age of 2. As the sample grew, and we observed more and more children, we learned a great deal about language development in the second year of life. As a result, we were in a position to recognise that three of the children in the larger sample that we were observing—all boys—had relatively slow language development.

As we had been recording these children with their mothers regularly since the age of 6 months, it was possible to compare the early language experience of the three slow developers with that of the children who had taken part in the first study (a full report of this second study appears in Harris, Jones, Brookes & Grant, 1986).

Language Assessment at 2 Years

The first step, however, was to confirm our informal observation that the language development of the three children was relatively slow. The study had not originally been concerned with children's language development and so there were no diary records on which to base estimates of the children's vocabulary; and we could not go back and test the language of the children in the original study as they were, by now, too old. So the best solution seemed to be to assess language development from our video-recordings.

It was decided that the language assessment should be derived from the video-recording that was made closest to the child's second birthday. Unfortunately, one of the original subjects had dropped out of the study at 19 months as his parents went abroad. This left a comparison between seven of the original subjects and the three new subjects.

Since it is by no means clear precisely what is the best measure of language development at 2 years, several measures were used. All were taken from a transcript of 10 continuous minutes of the recording of free play made in the observation room when the child was approximately 2 years old. The measures used were mean length of utterance in morphemes (MLU), mean length of 10 longest utterances (MLU10), length of longest utterance and the total number of different words produced. The range of measures was intended to sample both the length—and so, at this early stage of language development, the complexity—of the sentences that the children were producing and the range of their vocabulary.

As it turned out, there was no overlap in any of the measures of language development from the two groups of children. The MLU of the slower developers was 1.0 (range 1.0–1.1), whereas that of the normal developers was 1.9 (range 1.2–3.4). The MLU10 scores showed an even larger difference: The slower developers had a mean of 1.1 (range 1.0–1.2) compared with a mean score of 3.8 (range 1.9–7.9) for the normal developers. The longest utterances of the slower developers varied between 1.0 and 2.0 while, for the normal developers, the range was 3.0–12.0.

These comparisons show that, as it had initially appeared, the language of the slower developers really was less advanced. In essence, the three slower developers were producing almost exclusively single-word speech, whereas all of the normal developers were producing a significant number of multi-word constructions.

The vocabulary of the slower developers was also smaller. The total number of different words they used in 10 min ranged between 9 and 14. For the normal developers, the minimum number of words produced was 20 and the maximum was 77.

One can see from these statistics that there was considerable variation among the seven children from the original sample. This was not surprising, since these children had not been specially selected— they were just the first children on whom we had completed observation up to the age of 2 years. Some of the children had very sophisticated language but by no means all of them and, as such, they formed a very interesting comparison group for the three slower developers. What was of particular interest was whether the language experience of the three slower developers was actually different from that of the children in the original sample; and if it proved to be so, what would this suggest?

Analysis of the Interaction

As I mentioned in Chapter 4, there are serious methodological difficulties in examining the relationship between language input and language development. One of the most problematic areas is that of disentangling cause and effect, since the way that mothers talk to their children is influenced by the children's own language ability. In a larger sample, it would be possible to overcome part of this problem statistically (see Ellis & Wells, 1980; Gleitman et al., 1984), but with this small sample, and given the longitudinal nature of the observations and the use of videotape, it was decided to adopt another method. This was to go back in time from the point at which the children's language had been assessed to an earlier point when none of the children had any recognisable language. In this sample, such a point occurred when the children were 16 months old. (This was the main reason why the third assessment of maternal speech occurred at 16 months in the original study, since it was considered better to compare maternal language at various points before the children began producing words.)

At 16 months, none of the children in the sample was producing any recognisable words. They were all using certain phonetic forms relatively consistently, but the mothers did not consider these to be words. It was thus relatively unlikely that the mothers' own language was being influenced by what their children were saying. Of course, it is possible that there were some differences in the children's comprehension. But it is important to remember that the measures of maternal speech that were used in the first study were remarkably stable over a period of 6–16 months. So it is reasonable to assume that measures of maternal language at 16 months are reflecting something about the kind of language that a child has been exposed to from 6 months onwards—well before comprehension has started to develop. (I do not think that this would be true of all measures of maternal language. What is important is that a case can be made for the kinds of measures used here which tap the relationship between language and the non-verbal context.)

As I have already implied, the measures of maternal language that were used for the three slower developers at 16 months were those that had been used in the previous study. However, in addition, I decided to use a second measure of maternal utterances which provided a clearer picture of the precise relationship between what a mother was saying and its immediate context. My reason for doing so was this: If a child is going to be able to exploit the fact that words he/she is hearing are describing something in the environment, it is necessary that this relationship should be a very specific one. If it were not, and if words that a mother used in one context occurred in a very large number of different—and unrelated—contexts, then the child would have little idea about what the mother could be referring to. This problem is best understood in terms of references to objects. One should remember that these featured very prominently in maternal speech—so, for this reason too, they are an important case to consider.

There are various ways that someone might refer to an object. One way would be to use a specific label such as "teddy" or "car"; another way would be to use a general term such as a demonstrative ("that" or "this"), a pronoun ("it") or a word like "thing". The same goes for attributes of objects. An object might be referred to by colour or shape (which provides specific information) or it might be described as "interesting" or "pretty" (which does not). In the study, maternal references to objects were subdivided into those that contained at least one piece of specific information and those that did not. (Fortunately, mothers did not use superordinate terms, like "furniture", to refer to objects, and so this division was rather more straightforward than it might have been in the case of speech to adults.)

Results

As it turned out, the new measure of the specificity of object references in maternal speech proved to be the most interesting. But I will begin by describing the pattern that emerged when the original analysis was carried out with the three slower developers, since this provided the first indication of differences in the language experience of the two groups.

The episode analysis revealed that the overall structure of episodes was generally the same for the slower developers as it had been for the original subjects (see Table 5.9). In both groups, roughly two-thirds of episodes were child-initiated. The profile of types of initiation within child-initiated episodes was also very similar: initiations involving action predominated. However, there was an interesting difference for mother-initiated episodes. Although all of the mothers most commonly introduced a new episode with an accompanying action, the mothers of the slower developers were more likely to initiate a new episode without an accompanying action.

More differences emerged from the analysis of individual utterances, which is summarised in Table 5.10. In comparison to mothers of the slower developers, mothers of children with normal language

TABLE 5.9
Mean Proportions of Different Types of Episode Initiation
for Normal and Slower Developers

Sub-sample	Mother-initiated Episodes			Child-initiated Episodes				
	Verbal	Verbal + Gaze	Verbal + Action	Vocal'n	Gaze	Vocal'n + Gaze	Action	Vocal'n + Action
Normal developers	0.03	0.03	0.94	0.05	0.07	0.01	0.45	0.42
Slower developers	0.15	0.00	0.85	0.01	0.07	0.04	0.49	0.39

TABLE 5.10

Mean Proportions of Current and Potential References in Mothers' Speech
to Normal and Slower Developers at 16 Months

| | Sub-sample of Children | | | |
| | Slower Developers | | Normal Developers | |
Reference	Current	Potential	Current	Potential
Mother's action	0.03	0.03	0.03	0.01
Child's action	0.05	0.30	0.10	0.22
Object	0.49	0.29	0.74	0.07
Attribute	0.16	0.13	0.25	0.05

Note: The proportions for the normal developers are slightly different from those shown in Table 5.8 because only seven children were included in this sample.

development made significantly more references to objects that were at her child's current focus of attention and fewer references to potential objects. They also made fewer references to potential attributes of objects. (The difference for references to current attributes went in the same direction but it was not significant.)

The most striking difference between the two groups of mothers, however, was in their use of specific references to currently attended objects. Whereas, for the children with normal language development, almost half (46%) of the references were specific, only one-quarter of such references to the children with slower language development were specific.

Individual Differences in Maternal Style

The comparison of the language experience of the normal and slower developers pinpointed some interesting differences. These differences were, however, relatively subtle. As the episode analysis revealed, it was not that the mothers of the slower and normal developers were choosing to talk about different topics: all the mothers were structuring a majority of conversational topics around the child's activity. So, assuming that the children's language experience was having at least some influence on their early language development, what might have been going wrong in the case of the slower developers?

The short answer to this question is that there was a much less close relationship between maternal speech and the immediate non-verbal context in the language experience of the three slower developers, and this provided these children with fewer opportunities to note consistent links between words that they heard and objects and events to which they were attending. But, like most short answers, this does not get us very far. For it turns out that the reasons why the language experience of the slower developers presented them with fewer such opportunities were complex, and there were interesting individual differences in the maternal styles of the three mothers.

Consider possible reasons why what a mother is saying might not provide any specific information about an aspect of the child's immediate non-verbal environment. The first, and most obvious, possibility is that a mother does not talk about events and objects at the child's current focus of attention. As we have just seen, there was some evidence that was the case in this study. Overall, the mothers of the slower developers made fewer references to currently attended objects and more references to potential objects. But this does not explain *why* these mothers showed this pattern—a point I will take up in a moment—nor why one of the three mothers did, in fact, produce a relatively large number of references to current objects (72%).

As it turns out, the fact that one of the mothers of a slow developer produced such a large number of references to currently attended objects does not invalidate my claim that *all* the slow developers were provided with relatively few opportunities to observe relationships between maternal speech and the immediate non-verbal context. The explanation for this lies in a second reason why what a mother says may not provide specific information about the context: This is that, although she refers to objects on which the child is currently focusing attention, she does so by using general, rather than specific, terms. This proved to be the case for the one mother who made a large number of references to current objects: most of these references involved the use of general terms like "that one", "it" and "them".

The other two mothers showed an opposite pattern. Although they made relatively few references to current objects, almost all of these were specific. Strikingly, the net result of the two rather different maternal styles was identical. Twenty per cent of the first mother's utterances contained at least one specific reference to a currently attended object, while the corresponding figure was 21% for both of the other two mothers. (Overall, twice as many utterances to the normal developers contained at least one specific reference.)

The reader may wonder why two of the mothers produced so few references to currently attended objects. Close re-analysis of the video-recordings revealed that this came about because of a very slight asynchrony. The most common reason for this asynchrony was that the mother noted that her child was attending to a new object and commented on this. However, because she waited too long before commenting, the child had turned attention to a new activity by the time that the utterance occurred. The other, much less common, reason for asynchrony was that the mother attempted to direct the child's attention to a new object by commenting on it (and sometimes taking hold of it), but the child either failed to turn attention to the object or did so only after the utterance.

It would appear from our small sample, then, that maternal speech may contain relatively few examples of specific information about the currently attended context either because of a slight mistiming or because of the use of general rather than specific terms. One can probably think of ways in which these two patterns might be remediated, but I probably still need to persuade you that these differences between the styles of the mothers of the slower developers and those of the normal developers were actually contributing to the differential rates of language development. After all, although there were significant differences between the two groups and even though the sample of interaction analysed was taken at a point when the language development of all three children appeared very similar, there might be some common explanation for differences both in maternal style and children's language development. In particular, it is important to remember that the pattern of mother–child interaction is very significantly influenced by the child as well as by the mother.

I want to try and convince the reader of my argument mainly by considering in much more detail what the relationship is between early language development and early language experience (which I do in the next two chapters). However, I want to make just one more comment about maternal style. Two of the mothers of the children, who later turned out to have slower language development, had clear ideas about what their main aims were in interacting. They spontaneously expressed the view that they were encouraging their children—both of whom were boys—to be independent and, as a result, the children were encouraged to play on their own. As one might guess, it was these two mothers who produced such a small number of references to currently attended objects.

CHAPTER SIX

Language Experience and Vocabulary Development

In the previous chapters, I have argued that the early stages of children's language development are firmly rooted in their experience of adult speech being used in a familiar social-interactional context. In Chapter 5, I made a stronger claim, namely, that a child's early language development may actually be delayed if he/she has few opportunities to observe particular words being consistently used in familiar interactional contexts.

The research that I have described so far provides some support for this claim. However, it does not offer an explanation of exactly why language experience of a certain kind might be important for early language development. As I hinted in the last chapter, I think that the only way forward in this area is to try to develop specific accounts of the relationship between language experience and particular aspects of language development. In other words, it is necessary to stop talking about early language development in general and to begin to consider the various stages of development individually.

The most logical place to start is early vocabulary development. There are various reasons for this. Initially, I was driven to consider early vocabulary development because, in reading the literature in this area, I found the counterpart of many of the views that I had developed through my research into maternal speech. Most notably, I was attracted by the notion that children's early use of words is often highly restricted—under-extended—by adult standards. This seemed compatible with the view that children initially base their own use of words on their experience of hearing an adult use a word in one particular context.

There are, however, other reasons for considering vocabulary development as a likely area where language experience will have a strong influence. One concerns the arguments that I set out in Chapter 1 about the need to separate considerations of lexical and syntactic development from the viewpoint of innate processes. Another stems from the research into the social context of early language development that I discussed in Chapter 3. The weaker version of Bruner's theory (Bruner, 1983a, 1983b) is no longer concerned with grammatical forms. Instead, it views the child's socio-linguistic experience as facilitating the linguistic expression of communicative intent—an expression that is initially realised through the early stages of developing a vocabulary.

There is one final reason for considering the relationship between early lexical development and language experience. This is that studies considering the relationship between adult speech and syntactic development have, with a small number of exceptions, yielded negative results; and such relationships as do exist are by no means clear-cut. A priori, there is no reason why the same should prove to be true of lexical development and, particularly, its early stages.

For a variety of reasons, then, I became interested in the relationship between early lexical development and language experience. And, for the same reasons, when I first began my research in this area I was convinced that a study of the relationship between lexical development and maternal speech would provide an acid test of the hypothesis that language development is influenced by the child's socio-linguistic experience. If no relationship were detectable, then I was prepared to give up this hypothesis.

The reader will, however, have to wait until the next chapter to find out whether I had to make such an intellectual sacrifice because, in order to be able to make clear predictions about what relationship—if any—exists between children's lexical development and the speech they hear, it is essential to know something about vocabulary development. Fortunately, there is a wealth of literature on this topic and, in the next section, I present a brief overview of some of the key ideas that have emerged from the very extensive research that has been carried out (readers who are particularly interested in this topic will find more detailed reviews in Barrett, 1986, 1989; Nelson, 1988).

VOCABULARY DEVELOPMENT

One immediate striking feature of the lexical development literature is that there is a very great discrepancy between the amount of research into lexical comprehension and lexical production. Only a relatively small number of studies have been concerned with what children understand words to mean, whereas a very large number have studied how children use words. This discrepancy is particularly apparent in the case of studies of lexical development in the first 2 years of life. It is important to bear this in mind when considering accounts of lexical development. For the most part, they are really accounts of the development of production, although there is often an assumption that there is an isomorphism between production and comprehension. This is a point that I will return to later in this chapter. However, for the moment, I want to consider what we know about the course of lexical development.

One feature of recent views about vocabulary development is an increasing emphasis on the existence of distinct developmental periods. Various researchers (notably, Barrett, 1986; Nelson & Lucariello, 1985; Nelson, 1988) have identified three such periods.

Phase One

The first period is one in which the child attempts to find a way into language. It begins when the child first begins to show signs of understanding some of the language that he/she hears by responding in a consistent way when certain words or phrases are used. Such signs of understanding may occur well before the end of the first year of life, although, at this very early age, it is sometimes difficult to be certain whether a child is responding to what is said or to some more general—non-verbal—aspects of the situation in which the words are used. Rigorous testing, however, has shown that some children can respond appropriately to words or phrases, independently of their wider non-verbal context, when they are as young as 7 months (Gunzi, unpublished; Harris, Yeeles & Oakley, 1991).

The first phase of development continues until the point at which the child is able to produce 30 or more different words and also begins to produce the first two-word combinations. Typically, there is a considerable lag between production and comprehension. Children can usually understand many words before they start to produce their first word, although there are considerable differences among children in this respect both in the number of words understood and in the number of months intervening between the onset of comprehension and that of production. In a study by Harris et al. (1991) of eight children, one child, Katherine, understood her first word at 7 months and understood a total of 26 words before she produced her first word at 11 months. In contrast, Ben, another child in the same study, who also understood his first word at 7 months, built up a comprehension vocabulary much more slowly than Katherine: 5 months later, when he produced his first word, he understood only seven words. Bates et al. (1988) and Gunzi (unpublished) also report considerable variation in the lag between production and comprehension.

As one might expect, there is also considerable variation in the age at which a child can produce 30 different words. Some children produce very few words before the age of 18 months; others begin to use words when they are under 1 year of age and can produce 30 different words by the time they are 15 months old.

Nelson (1988) argues that this initial period of lexical development can be characterised as an attempt by the child to discover what words are and what they can do. In particular, the child is attempting to find out how words can be used to refer and whether a single word can be used to refer to more than one category of things or events.

A general indication of the initial difficulty that the child has in coming to terms with what it is that words do is the fact that the learning of first words is a very slow process: up to 5–6 months may elapse between the production of the first word and the production of the tenth (Harris, Barrett, Jones & Brookes, 1988; Harris et al., 1991). More specific evidence of the child's struggle to find the answers to the questions described by Nelson can be derived from an analysis of cases where a child's use of a word is different from that of an adult.

There has been considerable debate about the best way to characterise children's idiosyncratic word use in the early period of development. The first studies placed particular emphasis on cases where a child used a word in a way that an adult would consider too general, and reports of "over-extension"—as such use is described—abound in the literature (see, for example, Barrett, 1986; Bowerman, 1976; Lucariello, 1987; Rescorla, 1980). Among the examples given by Rescorla (1980) is the use of "clock" to refer to real clocks and watches, meters, dials, timers, bracelets, a buzzing radio and telephone and a chevron-shaped medallion. And, probably the most famous example of all, is the case described by Bowerman (1976), in which a child used the word "moon" to refer to a grapefruit half, lemon slices and a hangnail.

Theories of the underlying reasons for patterns of over-extension have proved controversial and the most plausible account is almost certainly that there is no single basis for over-extension (see Barrett,

1986; Nelson, 1988). More significantly from my own standpoint, the last decade of research has seen the discussion of over-extension being counterbalanced by an increasing number of reports of under-extended word use (see, for example, Barrett, 1986; Bates et al., 1979; Dore, 1985; Nelson & Lucariello, 1985). There is now considerable support for the view that under-extension, rather than over-extension, is typical of word use at the start of production.

There are two different kinds of under-extension. The most well-documented is the case of "context-bound" word use in which a child produces a word only in a limited and specific context (and not in other contexts where an adult would consider the use of the word to be appropriate). Some of the best known examples of context-bound use come from Barrett (1986), where his son, Adam, is reported as using the word "duck" only when hitting a toy duck off the edge of the bath and "chuff-chuff" only when pushing a toy train along the floor. Other typical cases are the use of the word "hello" only when a child was holding a telephone receiver to her ear (Harris et al., 1991), the use of "bye" only when a child was replacing a telephone receiver (Bates et al., 1979) and the use of "go" only when a child was taking his mother over to a door (Barrett, Harris, Jones & Brookes, 1986).

A somewhat different kind of early under-extension has also been reported. This is the use of a word that is restricted, not to a particular situation, but to a particular referent or subset of referents (irrespective of the situation in which they occur). Under-extension of this kind is not context-bound but contextually flexible and it would appear that, in cases of this kind, children are using words in a way that is genuinely referential. Examples of this kind of contextually flexible under- extension are relatively sparse in the literature, but I have encountered several such cases in my own research. For example, in Harris et al. (1991), I describe early uses of "clock" to refer only to wall clocks, "music" to refer only to a hi-fi system in the child's home, and "light" to refer only to ceiling lights with a conventional shade. And in Barrett et al. (1986), we report the use of the word "teddy" by James initially to refer only to one particular teddy.

There is also evidence that, even at the outset of lexical development, some words are used referentially to refer to a range of appropriate exemplars. Strictly speaking, of course, such words could theoretically still be relatively under-extended: the critical distinction here is between a word that is used only for one—or a very small subset—of exemplars and one which is used for a large number of exemplars. Examples of highly flexible word use of this kind appear in Bates et al. (1979), where one of their subjects is reported as using the word "ball" to name any ball and another as using "dog" right from the outset to name both toy dogs and real dogs.

These various different kinds of early word use raise a number of issues about the likely relationship between lexical production in phase one and language experience. I will explore these in the second section of this chapter. What I want to do now is to compare phase one of lexical development with phase two.

Phase Two

The second period of lexical development begins when the child can produce about 30 words. It is most noticeably characterised by a very marked increase in the speed with which new words are acquired—the so-called "vocabulary explosion". The most common explanation for this marked increase in the rate of lexical development is that it occurs because the child has learned that things have names (Dore, 1978; McShane, 1979; Nelson, 1973).

As I will argue later, this may be too simple an explanation, but it is clear that something fairly radical occurs in the way that children go about acquiring new words once they have learned 30 or so words. One overt sign of the change is that children start to ask for the names of objects and they also go around labelling everything for which they do know the name. Another is that children become capable of "fast mapping", that is, acquiring a word on a single exposure. Experimental studies by Nelson and Bonvillian (1978) into the acquisition of novel object names and by Carey and Bartlett (1978) into the acquisition of novel colour names have shown that children in phase two of lexical development are capable of learning a new word after having heard it being used only once.

It is not yet clear whether the phenomenon of fast mapping extends beyond the case of object and colour names, although there is reason to suppose that is does because of the very rapid rate at which children learn new words towards the end of phase two.

Nelson (1988) suggests that what distinguishes the second phase of vocabulary development from the first is that, in the first phase, children are trying to discover what words are used for whereas, in the second phase, they have discovered this: they have learned about the conceptual categories that describe things and events in the world and have realised that words can be used to refer to these categories. Thus, in the second phase of lexical development, children know (in general terms) about the kinds of meanings that words can have and so they are able to take active steps to discover the words that are attached to these meanings. Nelson points out, however, that children in phase two work on the assumption that there is a one-to-one relationship between concepts and words. In other words, they assume that if they hear a word, then there must be a single concept to which it relates and, conversely, if they have a concept, then there is a single word that can be used to describe it.

Much of the time, this assumption of a one-to-one correspondence between words and concepts is an appropriate one. However, there are several areas where it is not and many well-known examples of children's persisting difficulty in acquiring words during phase two can usefully be subsumed under the notion of a general difficulty of the kind that Nelson suggests. For example, Karmiloff-Smith (1979) has described the change that takes place in children's understanding of terms which have no one-to-one correspondence with a concept as a move from treating each word as having only one function to treating words as plurifunctional. For example, a word like "same" can refer either to identity (same one) or similarity (same kind). Until the age of about 5 years, a child understands "same" only in the similarity sense, which is correct in a situation where two different things are being compared (as in "Are these the same?"), but incorrect in the expression, "the same X". Before 5, a child will incorrectly treat such usage as referring to "another X with the same attributes". By the age of 5, however, children acquire the identity sense of "same" and realise that in the expression "the same X", the word "same" actually means "one and the same".

Other well-known examples come from studies of children's understanding of comparative terms like "more" and "less" (Donaldson & Wales, 1970) and superordinates (Nelson, 1983). Here, the general problem for the child seems to be a difficulty in grasping the notion that meaning is, in some sense, relational. And, in such cases, there is no simple concept–word relationship.

As the reader will by now have realised, the second period of vocabulary development lasts for several years as the child builds up an extensive knowledge of words and their associated conceptual distinctions. However, as we have just seen, some ares of lexical knowledge remain incomplete and important changes in the organisation of the lexicon and, particularly, in the relationship between words and concepts, take place in the final phase of development.

Phase Three

The third phase of lexical development is a period of revision, reorganisation and consolidation of knowledge. It normally begins in the early preschool years (when the child is aged 3–4) and is marked by extremely rapid word learning. Children commonly learn between 10 and 20 new words every day during the preschool period and parents often report their astonishment at how many words their child knows.

Careful experimentation has shown that the problems with comparative, superordinate, deictic and plurifunctional terms that characterised phase two are gradually overcome (see Karmiloff-Smith, 1979; Donaldson & Wales, 1970). This suggests that, in phase three, the child is reorganising the lexicon in two different—but closely related—ways. One is the reorganisation of lexical items into domains of related words, which allows the child to represent information about relationships between individual words. The other is the development of a more complex mapping between words and word domains on the one hand and concepts on the other. This allows the child to represent relationships other than those in which there is a one-to-one correspondence between word and concept (see Nelson, 1988, for a more extensive discussion of the changes in phase 3).

EARLY VOCABULARY DEVELOPMENT AND MATERNAL SPEECH

One way of viewing the changes in vocabulary development is to see the child as developing more and more lexical structure. Initially, at the start of phase one, the child does not know anything about words and so each word is acquired independently of other words. By the time the child can produce about 30 words, he/she has begun to develop a primitive level of meta-representation. That is, the child extracts some general principles about the kinds of meaning that words have. This meta-representation informs the acquisition of subsequent words, for now the child has a basis on which to discover the names for objects and certain kinds of event that he/she encounters.

As we have seen, the child's meta-representation continues to develop throughout phases two and three and this allows the reorganisation of individual words into increasingly complex systems of related items. Unfortunately, a detailed discussion of this level of reorganisation is beyond the scope of this book and all I want to point out here is that, hand in hand with notions of increasing lexical structure and the development of increasing levels of meta-representation, is the idea of an increasing reliance on internally driven processes and decreasing reliance on externally driven ones.

Turning this argument on its head, it follows that lexical development is most likely to be sensitive to external factors at its outset, that is, at the point where the child is learning what it is that words do and where each word is acquired independently. Thus, the most appropriate point at which to consider whether there is a relationship between vocabulary development and language experience is the outset of development. For this reason, the main study that I report in this chapter investigated the first 10 words that children produced.

As I have already noted in my discussion of phase one of lexical development, children typically use their earliest words in a relatively restricted way. In the limiting case of context-bound words, their initial use of a word is restricted to only one specific situation. And in the case of under-extension of object names, a word is initially applied only to one exemplar (or a small subset) of a class of objects.

Such limitation of word use is, however, very unlikely to be a feature of adult speech, even of maternal speech to young children. This difference between adult and early child use of words raises an interesting question. If children are, as I have claimed, influenced by their experience of hearing words being used and, if they actually derive their own word use from their experience of adult use, then it is important to consider what factors lead a child to model his or her own use on one adult use rather than another.

I argued in the last chapter that young children require the opportunity to observe consistent links between words that they hear and objects and events to which they are already attending. One important element of consistency is frequency. Thus, one factor that is likely to determine which of several adult uses the child will use as a basis for his or her own production is relative frequency.

In case you are wondering whether my claims about relative frequency are informed by the results of the research that I will shortly be describing, I should perhaps point out that I originally set out this argument in Harris et al. (1984/5). There I pointed out that the child's first task in the very early stages of learning to produce words is to select one context from the many different contexts in which a given word is spoken by others when interacting with the child. And I suggested that what would make one particular context of adult word use salient for the child was the fact that it occurred frequently.

I argued that the selection of one context of use was necessary before a child could extract information about the relationship between a word and the context in which it is used. Given what I now know about early vocabulary development, I think that my argument was wrong in one respect, namely, that the child does not always select only one context as the basis for early word use. However, as we will see, whether the child selects only one context or more than one, relative frequency appears to be an important factor.

Since the study described in the next chapter was concerned with early lexical development, its aim was not only to look at the relationship between children's early word use and maternal speech, but also to carry out a systematic analysis of the different kinds of word use that were evident in the first 10 words produced by the children in the study. As I have already noted, several authors have claimed that children's first words are always context-bound (Barrett, 1986; Bates et al., 1979; Dore, 1985; Nelson & Lucariello, 1985). Indeed, Nelson (1988) describes this as "a position endorsed by many if not most of the observers of early child language". As I have also noted there are, however, a small number of observations of very early referential word use (notably in Bates et al., 1979), and this suggests that not all early word use is context-bound. The second aim of the study was to determine whether this was the case.

CHAPTER SEVEN

The Establishment and Development of Word Meaning

STUDY 3:
RELATIONSHIPS BETWEEN MATERNAL
SPEECH AND CHILDREN'S FIRST WORDS

Data Collection

This study was carried out in collaboration with Martyn Barrett and David Jones and various aspects of the data from it are described in Barrett et al. (1986), Harris (1987), Harris et al. (1988), Harris and Barrett (1989), Barrett, Harris and Chasin (1991) and Harris (1992).

The methodology of the study was essentially very similar to that used in the two studies described in the previous chapter. We observed four first-born children from the age of 6 months to 2 years. There were three girls, Jacqui, Jenny and Madeleine, and one boy, James. The children and their mothers came regularly to the video laboratory at Birkbeck College where they were filmed for 20 min while engaged in free play. For the first 4 months of the study, filming took place every month. Once the children were 10 months old, filming took place every 2 weeks.

Since the study was concerned with early vocabulary development, we also asked the mothers to keep diary records on prepared sheets which they brought with them when they came for a filming session. The diary records were used to note any new words that the child produced and any new uses of existing words, together with detailed information about the context in which each use had occurred. Initially, the mothers were often unsure about the amount of information that they should provide but detailed discussion of early entries clarified this point. The diary records, together with the fortnightly video-recordings, were used to identify the first 10 words used by each of the children.

Analysis of Word Use

Children's Initial Word Use

The first stage in the analysis was to identify the first 10 words used by each of the children. This was a painstaking task because, as I have already indicated, children seldom use words in an adult way at the outset of development, and so it was essential to keep an open mind about what an early use might be like. A further complication is that, in this early period, children's words often do not even sound like an adult word, since their phonological abilities are relatively immature.

Because of these problems, it was necessary to have a relatively open-ended definition of a word that took account both of maternal reports in the diary records and the child's behaviour during the observation sessions. In essence, it was decided to use two alternative criteria. The first was a maternal report of a word that was supported by at least *one* laboratory observation. The maternal report and the observation had to be consistent—although not identical—both in terms of the sound of the word and the context in which it was used.

Since it seemed unlikely that all early words would be reported by the mothers—simply because they are often so difficult to identify—the second criterion involved only laboratory observations. Here, the criterion was that *three* instances should be observed with all three having roughly the same phonetic form and occurring in behaviourally consistent contexts.

The notion of a behaviourally consistent context was an important part of both criteria. Its purpose was to distinguish a sound that was actually a word from other frequently used sounds that were not words. The critical distinction is that, in the case of a word, there should be some coherence to the contexts of use whereas, for other frequently used sounds that are not words, the pattern of use should be essentially random.

A final point to note is that, in all cases, the instances that were used were of the child's *spontaneous* production of a word. Cases where a child was imitating the mother's use of a word were excluded. It was, of course, relatively easy to tell from the video-recordings whether a child's vocalisation was an imitation. (I say, "relatively easy", because even here it took some time to come up with an operational definition of imitation.)

In the case of maternal reports, it might have been more difficult to identify imitative uses; therefore, when we were discussing the early records with each mother, we explained that it was important to know whether or not she had just said a word before the child said it. Fortunately, we found that mothers were very reliable in providing us with this information.

Children's Subsequent Word Use

As you would expect, the children's use of many of the words that were identified changed over the course of the study. Although the original aim had been to consider only initial uses of words, additional funding made it possible to consider second uses as well. The diary records and video-recordings were, therefore, inspected to see whether, for each of the 40 words, there was a change in use.

The criterion for identifying a second use was less stringent than for initial uses in that either a single maternal report or a single laboratory observation was taken as sufficient. The main reason why it was considered appropriate to rely on only one occurrence was that previous studies of changes in the use of individual words have shown that there is normally a very close relationship between the form and context of use of initial and subsequent uses (see Barrett, 1986, 1989). Therefore, once a word use is established, it is possible to use information both about the sound of that word and the general context of use as a cue to new uses.

Mothers' Word Use

There was only one available source of information about the mothers' word use, namely, their speech during the fortnightly observation sessions. In a world of limitless resources, it might have been possible to obtain samples of maternal speech in the home. However, I do not think that using a wider sample would necessarily have made the study any better for, as I have shown in the previous chapter, a very marked feature of a mother's language to her child is its consistency across time and situation. It thus seemed highly likely that the language that was recorded in the laboratory would actually reflect the language that the child was hearing at home. In any case, the sampling restriction made it less likely, rather than more likely, that there would be a detectable relationship between the children's word use and that of their mothers; and I was brought up to believe that, when in doubt, it is no bad thing to weight the odds against confirming a hypothesis.

The first step in using the video-recordings of the fortnightly observation sessions was to make transcriptions of the mother's speech at each session. Then, once a child's initial use of a word had been identified, all maternal uses of that same word were extracted from the two sessions immediately preceding the date at which the child's use of that word had been confirmed. (In cases where a child's word use was confirmed in an observation session, maternal word uses up to the point in that session where the confirmatory child use had occurred were also extracted.)

There were two reasons for deciding to focus on maternal speech in the two sessions immediately preceding identification of the child's use. The first is obvious and concerns the decision to analyse maternal speech from immediately preceding sessions: Once a child starts to use a word—particularly in the early stages of vocabulary development when most parents are anxiously listening out for their child's first words—it is quite likely that this will have an effect on the way that the mother uses that word. The second is less obvious—since it is, in some sense, arbitrary—and concerns the choice of transcripts from the *two* preceding sessions as the unit of analysis, that is, maternal speech from a period beginning roughly 1 month before the child's use of a word was confirmed. It would certainly have been possible to go back over a longer period, but the decision to go back 1 month was taken because of an intuition that, for the child, the most significant maternal uses of a word would be ones that had occurred relatively recently. (This relates to the distinction between input and uptake that I discussed in Chapter 4.)

Once the maternal uses of each of the children's 10 first words had been identified, a detailed behavioural description of the context of each instance of use was made. At this point in the analysis, any instances of use where the child was clearly not attending to the mother were excluded. Attended maternal uses were then grouped according to type—using the same general principles for grouping as were used in the identification of the children's words, that is, similarity of behavioural context—so that the number of different uses could be determined. Finally, the relative frequency of each use was determined.

The same procedure was then repeated for all children's second uses of words. All maternal uses of a word were extracted from the two sessions immediately preceding the appearance of the child's second use, and the relative frequency of different uses determined.

Results

The simplest way to describe the results of this study is to begin with a discussion of the children's use of words. As this is not the main focus of interest here, my discussion of this aspect of the findings will be relatively brief. A more extensive discussion of the findings—and their theoretical significance for theories of early lexical development—may be found in Harris et al. (1988) and Barrett et al. (1991).

Initial Use of Words by the Children

There was considerable variation in the age at which each of the four children in the sample produced his/her first word. The first word of the most precocious child appeared at 10 months (0:10.12) and that of the least precocious at nearly 16 months (1:3.23). There was a corresponding difference in the age at which the tenth word appeared although, on average, about 5 months elapsed between production of the first and tenth words.

It will be remembered that a vocalisation counted as a word if it was used by the child in a consistent behavioural context. The main reason for adopting a notion of consistency, rather than one of identity, was to allow for cases where a child's initial use of a word was contextually flexible. As it turned out, there were several cases of such flexible usage, but there were also cases of a word being used in only one behavioural context and it is with these cases that I will begin.

I have already described the concept of a *context-bound* word, so it is only necessary to say here that a word was assigned to this category if the three instances of use that were observed (or two in the case of a maternal report) were sufficiently similar to suggest that the child was using the word in only one specific context. This may sound a little vague as a definition but, in practice, what characterised context-bound words was that the children always accompanied their production with the same action. For example, Jenny initially used "choo-choo" only while she was pushing a toy train along the floor.

Contextually flexible words were, by contrast, used in at least two different behavioural contexts. There were two patterns of flexible use. The first involved reference to one particular object (or class of objects) and was categorised as *nominal* word use. The second pattern of contextually flexible use was more complex in that it did not involve reference to one particular object but, rather, reference to two or more contexts that shared some element in common. For convenience, these words will be referred to as *non-nominals*, but they should probably be thought of as more like nominals than context-bound words because of their contextual flexibility.

Table 7.1 gives some examples of the three different patterns of initial word use shown by the children in the sample. It will be seen there that, as I hinted earlier in this chapter, there are differences within the nominal class in the range of objects initially referred to by the child. Whereas "teddy" was initially used only in the presence of one particular teddy, "shoes" was used right from the outset to refer to various different shoes. The initial flexibility of use is even more striking in the case of non-nominals. There was considerable variation in the different contexts in which the word "more" was initially used, as Table 7.1 indicates.

TABLE 7.1
Examples of Children's Early Word Use

Type of Word	Word	Behavioural Context(s) of Initial Use
Context-bound	Mummy	C handing toy to M
	choo-choo	C pushing toy train along floor
Nominal	teddy	C sitting on big teddy
		C pointing at reflection of big teddy in mirror
	shoes	C looking at picture of shoes in book
		C pointing at own shoes
		C holding doll's shoes
Non-nominal	more	C reaching into toy box to take out more bricks
		C reaching to take another drink from cup
		C holding out empty bowl at meal time

Key: C = child; M = mother.

All four of the children used both contextually flexible and context-bound words. Overall, 22 of the total of 40 words were context-bound, 14 were nominals and 4 were non-nominals. Table 7.2 shows the words produced by each of the four children. [A complete list of the initial context(s) of use for each word appears in the appendix of Harris et al., 1988.]

Mothers' Word Use and its Relationship to the Children's Initial Word Use
As expected, preliminary analysis of the mothers' own use of a word in the two sessions before that word was produced by the child revealed that maternal word use was highly contextually flexible. Only six of the words were used by mothers in a single behavioural context. One such word was "boo", which was used by James' mother only when James was hiding behind a curtain in the observation room and they were playing peekaboo. The remaining 34 words were used in a variety of different contexts.

There was considerable variation in the number of different uses of the contextually flexible words. Some were used in only two different ways, many were used in at least three, and one word—"there" used by James' mother—occurred in 12 different situations. These included pointing up at a picture on a frieze, pointing at pictures in a book and talking into the receiver of a toy telephone. (A summary of the maternal uses of each word is given is the appendix of Harris et al., 1988.)

Having established the pattern of maternal word use for each of the words produced by the child, the child's use and the mother's use were compared. For each word, maternal uses were inspected to see whether

TABLE 7.2
The First 10 Words Produced by the Children
Grouped According to Pattern of Initial Use

Initial Use	Child			
	James	Jacqui	Jenny	Madeleine
Context-bound	mummy	wee	choo-choo	there
	go	hello	bye-bye	hello
	quack	mummy	there	here
	there	here		bye-bye
	buzz	no		
	moo	down		
	boo	more		
		go		
Nominal	teddy	Jacqui	teddy	teddy
	ball	bee	doggy	shoes
			moo	brum
			shoe	woof
			car	baby
Non-nominal	more		mummy	yes
			no	

any of them closely resembled the child's use. The notion of "close resemblance" is, of course, a crucial one in this study, and it is best illustrated with some examples. Table 7.3 gives four typical examples of the child's initial use of a word and the analogous maternal use (or uses).

Although the four examples shown in Table 7.3 are typical, they were not chosen at random. Each one illustrates a slightly different relationship between the child's word use and the mother's. In the case of "hello" (used by Jacqui), both mother and child used the word in exactly the same situation, that is, when the child was speaking into a toy telephone. In the case of "mummy" (used by James), the mother's use occurred when she was holding her hand out to take a toy from James while James used "mummy" when he was holding out a toy for his mother to take. (In case the reader is wondering why James' mother used the word "mummy" in this situation, it was because, when she held out her hand to take a toy from James, she often asked, "Is that for mummy?")

You will probably have noticed that both "hello" and "mummy" were initially used in a context-bound way by Jacqui and James. For context-bound words, it is relatively straightforward to decide whether there is a relationship between child and maternal word use. If there is

TABLE 7.3

Examples of Resemblance Between a Child's Initial Use of a Word and the
Mother's Use of the Same Word

Word	Child's Initial Use	Mother's Most Similar Use(s)
hello	C speaking into telephone receiver	C speaking into telephone receiver
mummy	C handing toy to M	M holds out hand to take toy from C
teddy	C labelling big teddy	M pointing at/holding big teddy C playing with/touching big teddy
no	C refusing drink C crawling to step which she is forbidden to climb down C refusing to comply with M's request	M prohibiting C from sucking toy M commenting on C's refusal C trying to put shape in wrong hole

Key: C = child; M = mother.

a relationship, there should be a close resemblance between the child's initial use of a word and *one* maternal use, since the child is only using a word in one specific situation. And, as the first two examples in Table 7.3 illustrate, this proved to be the case.

The nature of the relationship between maternal word use and an initial use by the child that is contextually flexible is necessarily more complex. In the case of a child's initial nominal use of a word, what one would expect if there is a relationship with maternal usage, is that both mother and child will use the word to refer to the same referent or class of referents. An example of this kind of close resemblance between the child's and mother's word use is Jenny's use of "teddy", shown in Table 7.3. Here, Jenny used the word to refer only to one particular teddy and her mother also used "teddy" to refer to the same teddy in a variety of situations.

The most complex relationship between the child's initial use of a word and maternal word use occurred for the four non-nominals. Here the child was using the word to refer to a number of different situations which shared some element in common. The critical question here was whether both mother and child used a word in the same range of situations. As can be seen from Table 7.3, in the case of "no" (used by Jenny) this was clearly the case. Jenny's use was associated with situations of non-compliance, prohibition or refusal. There were precedents for all three kinds of use in her mother's speech.

Overall, for the 40 initial word uses that were identified, there were only three cases where there was no relationship between the child's use and any of the maternal uses. One such case was Jenny's use of "mummy". Jenny used this word only when she wanted a cuddle from her mother: In the sample of maternal speech that we obtained from the preceding video-recordings, her mother used "mummy" twice when taking about her nose and once when pointing to her reflection in the mirror.

In the remaining 37 cases, there was a close resemblance between the child's initial word use and mother's use. What was even more striking—and unexpected—was that, in 33 cases, the child's initial use of a word was related to the mother's most frequent use or uses. That is, where the mother used a word in a variety of different ways, the child typically based his/her own initial word use on the maternal use that had occurred most frequently in the preceding month.

I will return to the significance of this finding later but, for the moment, it is worth noting that a consideration of the child's experience of maternal word use very often explained an otherwise mysterious initial use by the child. I have already mentioned the case of James' use of "mummy", which initially occurred only when he was handing a toy to his mother. Another interesting case was Jacqui's use of "go". She used "go" only when looking at a particular toy car immediately after her mother had activated the mechanism that made it move. It turned out that her mother had exclusively used "go" to Jacqui in exactly the same situation.

Children's Subsequent Use of Words
Analysis of the children's subsequent uses of words also provided some very interesting results. Since there were a large number of cases of initially contextually flexible use, one may not be surprised to learn that, for 11 of the words, there was no change in use over the observation period (up to the age of 2 years). The remaining words showed a variety of changes which are described in detail in Harris (1992) and Barrett et al. (1991).

As might be expected, the most significant changes occurred with words that were initially context-bound: only 3 of the total of 22 context-bound words showed no change over time. The others showed various kinds of extension of use and a total of nine became contextually flexible. For the nominals, the most common change was a broadening of referential scope. For the non-nominals, which might be thought of as the most contextually flexible, the most common pattern was for there to be no change in use. However, there was a change in use of the word "more". Some examples of the kinds of change in use that occurred are given in Table 7.4.

There is much that could be said about the theoretical significance of these changes in use and we discuss these at length in Barrett et al. (1991). What I want to concentrate on here, however, is the relationship between second uses of words and mothers' uses of these same words.

The Relationship Between Children's Second Uses of Words and Maternal Word Use

Although I had a clear idea about what external factors might influence the way that a child initially used a word, my thoughts about the relationship between changes in word use and maternal speech were far less clear. Essentially, there seemed to be two possibilities. One was that subsequent uses of words would, like initial uses, be strongly influenced by maternal word use. The other was that changes in use would mainly be driven by internal factors. In other words, once an externally derived initial use had been established, subsequent uses would be developed mainly on the basis of internally driven cognitive processes.

As it turned out, the results were not exclusively compatible with either of these possibilities. A significant number of second uses of words were closely related to maternal use but an even greater number were not. What was very striking, however, was that the very marked effect of frequency showed a dramatic decline.

The relationship between maternal word use and initial and subsequent child uses is summarised in Table 7.5. The most significant points to note are that there was no maternal precedent for over half the second uses, and in only one-quarter of cases was the second use related to the most frequent maternal use in the sampling period.

I think that these data reveal a great deal about the relationship between children's early word use and their language experience. But

TABLE 7.4
Examples of Changes in Word Use During the Observation Period

Type of Change in Use	Example	
Modification of context-bound word use	*boo*	I: C hiding behind curtain S: C hiding under cushion
Initially context bound, subsequently nominal	*mummy*	I: C handing toy to mother S: C cuddling mother
Broadening of referential scope of nominal	*teddy*	I: only to refer to big teddy S: to refer to both big and little teddy
Broadening of referential scope of non-nominal	*more*	I: to request or comment on recurrence of an object S: to request repetition of a set of actions

Key: C = child; M = mother; I = initial use; S = subsequent use.

TABLE 7.5
Relationship Between Children's Initial and Subsequent Word Uses
and Maternal Uses of the Same Words

Type of Relationship to Preceding Maternal Use	Children's Word Use	
	Initial	Subsequent
No relationship to any maternal use	3/40 (0.07)	16/29 (0.55)
Relationship to maternal use	37/40 (0.93)	13/29 (0.45)
relationship to most frequent maternal use	33/40 (0.83)	7/29 (0.24)
relationship to less frequent maternal use	4/40 (0.10)	6/29 (0.21)

before spelling out some of the implications of these findings, I should explain why I think that they can be taken on their face value and not dismissed as an artefact of the particular data that we collected.

Validity of the Sampling Procedure

In the previous chapter, I explained why I think that, in many cases, a relatively small sample of maternal speech obtained from a laboratory observation can be representative of the language that a child hears at home. One important consideration is that the mother is at home for a major part of the time with her child. Sampling maternal speech will not provide a good guide to a child's language experience in situations where he or she spends a large part of the day with another adult. Another important factor is the regular presence of other children. If a child has older siblings, who are at home all day, they will usually play a large part in any interactions. They will not only talk to the child, but they will also have a large influence on the pattern of interaction between the mother and the younger child (Woollett, 1986).

Because of these potentially confounding factors, all four children in the present study were first-borns and they had mothers who were at home with them full-time. Thus, there are good reasons for supposing that, in general, the sample of maternal speech that was obtained was representative of the children's language experience at home.

It is, however, important to consider whether the samples of maternal speech that were compared with initial and subsequent word uses by the child might have differed in the extent to which they were representative of language experience. If the samples used for subsequent uses were, for some reason, less representative, this might explain why such a relatively high proportion of second uses of words were unrelated to maternal speech. One possibility is that, whereas sampling maternal input provided an accurate picture of the child's total linguistic environment for initial uses of words, this was not true for subsequent uses, since it could be the case that, with increasing age, the child was exposed to linguistic input from other relatives and family friends.

At first sight, this is an explanation that needs to be given serious consideration but, on close inspection, it does not prove to be a worry. For, although second uses of individual words appeared later in development than initial uses, there was considerable overlap between the time periods in which initial and subsequent uses were first produced. This is because the second use of some words—particularly those that appeared early in development—actually appeared *earlier* than the initial use of some later words.

If this seems surprising, it should be remembered that, when children first start to produce words, their progress tends to be slow. For the four children in this study, there was a gap of up to 5 months between the appearance of the first word analysed and that of the tenth. It it also relevant to note that there were many instances where the second use of a word appeared only weeks after the initial use.

The same argument about the overlap in the time period in which initial and subsequent uses were produced also militates against the suggestion that the children in this study would have been capable of learning second uses of words on the basis of a single exposure. Were this the case, it could explain why so many second uses of words showed no relationship to maternal use. The problem would be that a single critical maternal utterance is very unlikely to be sampled in a fortnightly recording session.

Now, as I will point out in the next section, the child's sampling base for second uses does appear to be different. But this is not because second uses were developed at a point at which a child becomes capable of fast mapping, since this is a phenomenon that occurs somewhat later on in development (see Chapter 6).

THE CHANGING RELATIONSHIP BETWEEN MATERNAL WORD USE AND CHILDREN'S WORD USE

I hope I have been able to convince the reader that the results of the study described in this chapter provide an insight into the relationship between children's early lexical development and their language experience. What I want to do now is to consider the wider significance of the findings.

Establishing Production

The first issue to consider is what these findings reveal about children's initial use of words at the onset of production. There are several points to make. The first is that these data provide clear evidence that children use words in a variety of different ways right from the outset. All four children used some words in a context-bound way, that is, in only one specific situation. However, all four children also used some words in an initially contextually flexible way, that is, in at least two—and often more—different situations. This pattern of both initially context-bound and initially contextually flexible use has also been found by Dromi (1987) in her study of her daughter's vocabulary development (although Dromi also notes that context-bound words tend to occur more commonly in the first half of phase one of development than the second half).

At first sight, the fact that children appear to be capable of using words in an initially contextually flexible way so early in their production may appear surprising. But it is important to remember that production typically only begins once a child already understands a large number of words. And it seems likely that in many cases—and probably the majority—the production of a particular word will only occur once a child has already developed some understanding of that word.

A recent study by Gunzi (unpublished) of the vocabulary development of three children has shown that in all cases production of a word was preceded by comprehension some weeks or months earlier. Bates et al. (1988), however, have raised the possibility that some words may be produced *before* they are understood by the child and, if this is the case, it is interesting to speculate about how the prior comprehension history of a word might influence the way that a word is initially used in production. If a child does not understand a word at all, or only understands it in one context, then it is likely that the child's initial production of that word will be restricted to a single context. If, on the other hand, the child has a well-developed understanding of a particular word that is not restricted to a single context, it is likely that, when the child first produces that word, he or she will do so in a way that is contextually flexible.

I have some evidence from the observations of my nephew, Matthew, that this may be the case. Very fortunately, he was an extremely obliging infant and he was happy to have his comprehension of words continually probed by his aunt and his mother. (Since he and my sister, Catherine, afforded me such an ideal opportunity for testing out some of my hypotheses about early language development, I have dedicated this book to them.)

Testing Matthew's understanding of object names revealed that, in many cases, he was aware that they could be used to refer to a variety of different referents some months before he produced his first words. For example, when asked about "panda", he was able to point out pictures in books, a picture on a mug, the Worldwide Fund for Nature logo (which is a panda) and his panda-shaped haversack. He was also adept at finding a variety of examples of "clown" and, when asked, would point to several different clowns in a circus picture, a toy clown and also to the model clown on his bedroom lampshade. He was probably most expert in his pre-production knowledge of the meaning of "car". He showed signs of understanding that "car" referred to real cars on the road, pictures of cars (including formula one racing cars), cars on television and model cars. Not surprisingly, when Matthew first began to use the words "panda", "clown" and "car", he used all three in a contextually flexible manner.

It would appear, then, that early production of words is often underpinned by a relatively sophisticated understanding of the variety of situations in which particular words are used, and this explains why some words are used in a contextually flexible way right from the outset.

The way that a word is initially produced also appears to depend very significantly on the child's immediate experience of hearing that word being used by an adult. In the study described in the previous section, 37 out of the 40 words that were identified were initially used in a context (or contexts) that was identical to that used by the child's mother, and in 33 cases the child's initial use was the same as his/her mother's most frequent use.

What is not clear from the study is exactly how maternal word use was influencing the child's production. There are two possibilities. One is that the child's observation of maternal word use had a direct influence on production, that is, the child modelled his/her own initial use of a word on maternal word use. The other possibility is that maternal word use had an indirect influence via comprehension. That is to say, the child's experience of maternal word use determined the contexts in which a word was understood before production, and the pattern of comprehension then determined the initial pattern of production.

The data from this study do not, of course, provide any indication as to which of these interpretations is correct, and it is certainly possible that both types of influence may operate. There are, however, some pertinent findings from a recent study by Gunzi (unpublished), which investigated the effect of frequency of presentation on the acquisition of six novel object names (these were either nonsense words or low-frequency English words). The names were introduced into play sessions involving the novel objects which took place every fortnight from the time that the children were 10 months old. The children's mothers were instructed to use the object names only in the play sessions and half were spoken only once during a session (low-frequency) and the other half were spoken three times (high-frequency). The results showed that frequency of naming had a significant effect on acquisition. By the age of 21 months, all of the three high-frequency names were understood by all three children, whereas none of the low-frequency names was. What was particularly interesting , however, was that by the same age each child had learned to produce only one of the names suggesting that, even when a mother said a name three times per session, this was insufficient for a child to be able to master its production.

Subsequent unrestricted use of the unlearned names by the children's mothers had a dramatic effect on both comprehension and production. Once mothers were allowed to use the novel names as often as they wished, all three children rapidly mastered the comprehension of the remaining names and they also made considerable progress in their production of the names.

The results of Gunzi's experiment lend support to the view that children initially require considerable exposure to a word in order to establish both comprehension and production. They also suggest that, even after a word has been comprehended, a child may require considerable further experience of hearing that word being used in a consistent context before being able to produce it. The onset of vocabulary production is thus firmly rooted in the children's experience of adult speech. And, more particularly, it is rooted in the experience of hearing particular words frequently being used in particular contexts.

Extending the Use of Words

It would appear, however, that the development of second uses of early words is much less directly rooted in experience. Only 13/29 second uses of words had an immediate maternal precedent and in only 7/29 cases was the child's use the same as the mother's most frequent use. In the majority of cases, there was no maternal precedent for the child's second use.

The sharply different pattern of initial and subsequent uses strongly suggests that the processes by which the use of a word is initially established and those by which it is subsequently extended are significantly different. (I engage in some speculation about the nature of these differences in Chapter 9.) However, it remains an open question as to whether initial uses of *new* words, beyond the first 10, continue to be rooted in experience. I have a hunch that they do, and the hunch is supported by some evidence that comes from four of the second uses.

In order to simplify the argument up to this point, I have omitted to tell the reader about the fate of four of the words that were initially context-bound. These were "hello" (used by Jacqui), "bye bye" (used by Jenny), "there" and "bye bye" (both used by Madeleine). In all four cases, there was no detectable continuity between the initial use and the subsequent use. For example, Madeleine initially used "bye bye" only while talking into a toy telephone and later used it when waving goodbye to her father as he left for work in the morning. Jenny's use of "bye bye" was the mirror image of this: Her first use was associated with waving and her second with the use of a toy telephone.

From an adult perspective, these two uses of "bye bye" clearly have something in common, since they both involve an act of parting from someone. However, there is no reason to suppose that this overlap in meaning should be apparent to a young child particularly since, for the great majority of cases, second uses of words tended to be very closely related to first uses. It was, therefore, decided that the second uses of the four words mentioned above should be treated as the acquisition of a homonym, rather than as an extension of initial use. What is interesting about these four words—where the "second" use should more properly be thought of as a new first use—was that in all cases the subsequent use was identical to the most frequent maternal use in the sampling period. And this suggests that, while a second use may often not be directly related to prior maternal use, new first uses may continue to be so.

CONCLUSIONS

The results of this study support the view that the early stage of lexical development is firmly rooted in the child's experience of hearing particular words frequently being used in the same contexts. Furthermore, words that are salient to the child in this early stage are those in which the context of use actively involves the child. All of the 40 words that were identified in the study were initially used by the child when he/she was performing either a single action (in the case of context-bound words) or one of several actions (in the case of contextually flexible words). And the child's own action context was derived from experience of maternal word use in that same action context.

The pattern of second uses was different in that relatively few were modelled on the most frequent maternal use. Indeed, if the four cases of homonyms are excluded, there were only three instances of second uses stemming from the most frequent maternal use. One such was Jenny's second use of "car", which was initially used to refer to real cars and toy cars and was subsequently used to refer to pictures of cars in books. There were another six words for which there was at least one maternal precedent for the second use but the most common pattern was for there to be no maternal precedent for a second use.

In the final chapter of this book, I want to consider what this finding might imply for accounts of the kind of processing that underlie early vocabulary development. But, in order to be able to view this issue from a somewhat wider perspective, I first want to consider some of the recent research that has been carried out into the early vocabulary development of children who are born with a sensory handicap. This is because I think that an analysis of a developmental process that is occurring under somewhat abnormal circumstances can provide illuminating insights into essential characteristics of that process.

CHAPTER EIGHT

Early Language Development in Deaf Children

Children who are born with either severely impaired vision or hearing are confronted with very different problems in the early stages of language development. The blind child (with no other handicaps) can hear language perfectly normally but, in contrast to the experience of a sighted child, that language does not occur in a visually observable context. For blind children, the context of language is mediated through touch and, as I will argue in the next chapter, this makes some aspects of their early language experience rather different from that of a sighted child. Deaf children, on the other hand, have potentially full access to the visually observable context of language. But they have the problem that the language itself (be it sign language or spoken language) has to be perceived through the visual modality, and this may reduce the number of opportunities that are available to deaf children to observe both the language and—simultaneously—the context in which it is occurring.

These differences between the early experience of deaf and blind children suggest that the pattern of early language development in the two groups may be rather different if, as I have argued, lexical knowledge is at its outset firmly rooted in the child's social experience. What we might expect if we compare blind children with sighted children is that there will be some significant differences in the content of their early language development just because the two groups have a very different experience of hearing adults use words (see Chapter 9).

What we might expect in the case of deaf children is that they will develop language in much the same way as hearing children—since the content of their experience will be generally similar—but that they will show an initially slower rate of development since they have potentially fewer opportunities to relate language and context.

I want to discuss this latter possibility in this chapter and so I have chosen to focus upon recent research into the early vocabulary development of deaf children—concentrating, in particular, on a study of sign language development that I have recently completed—in order to consider what this can reveal about the role of language experience. The main purpose of this chapter is not to provide a comprehensive overview of research into the language development of deaf children, and readers who are more generally interested in this area will find reviews in Quigley and Paul (1984) and Wood, Wood, Griffiths and Howarth (1986).

LANGUAGE DEVELOPMENT IN DEAF CHILDREN

Variation in Language Development

The language development of deaf children varies enormously because of the large number of different factors that influence development. As one might expect, one of the most important factors is the extent and age of onset of hearing loss. Children whose hearing loss is profound or severe generally experience greater difficulty than those with only a moderate hearing loss. And children who are born deaf, or who become deaf in the first year of life, have considerably more difficulty in developing language than do children whose deafness is acquired later in life. It is difficult to be very precise about the significance of age of onset of hearing loss, since there are no large-scale studies of children whose deafness is acquired. However, the crucial point would appear to be whether a child is *prelingually* deaf.

Comparing hearing loss among children is by no means straightforward, not least because recent developments in the technology of hearing aids have resulted in the parameters of the various subdivisions of hearing loss being revised upwards. One particular problem is that hearing loss in the same individual is usually different at different frequencies of sound, and what is important for language is what the profile of loss is across the frequencies that are used in speech.

As will have been deduced from an earlier paragraph, hearing loss is normally subdivided into three categories. Profound hearing loss is an average loss of 90 dB or greater in the better ear (averaged across all frequencies), while a hearing loss is categorised as "severe" if it averages between 70 and 90 dB. A "severe/moderate" loss is one that is greater than 55 dB.

Apart from hearing loss, another factor that influences language development in deaf children is whether their parents are deaf or hearing. The great majority—about 95%—of deaf children are born to hearing parents (Kyle & Allsop, 1982), but several studies have shown that the small minority who have deaf parents generally outperform the majority on a variety of developmental measures including language development (Kampfe & Turecheck, 1987). Various suggestions have been offered for this. One suggestion is that deaf parents provide a more advantageous home environment because they have a much greater insight into the communicative needs of a deaf child, particularly in the early years (Gregory & Barlow, 1988; Swisher & Christie, 1988). Another points to differences in the kind of exposure to language that a deaf child receives at home and, later, at school.

Children who are born to deaf parents are often exposed to sign language from birth. Children born to hearing parents may be exposed to sign language from an early age—if their parents learn to sign—but will often first encounter sign language when they go to school. Other children of hearing parents may be exposed only to spoken language at both home and school.

There is thus considerable variation in the language experience of deaf children and so it is impossible—and certainly unwise—to make general statements about the language development of the deaf child (readers who are interested in this issue will find a comprehensive review in Quigley & Paul, 1984). However, the fact that a small group of children grow up in homes where sign language is used as the first language provides an ideal opportunity to investigate the development of a language that is manually rather than orally encoded.

Learning Sign Language

So far, I have talked very loosely about "sign language". In fact, there are many different sign languages just as there are many different spoken languages. The most extensive research has been carried out on the language used by the deaf community in the United States— American Sign Language (ASL)—but more recently there has been a growing body of research into British Sign Language (BSL).

Although all sign languages are different, they initially present the young child with a similar set of problems. I have shown in the previous chapters that the spoken language that children hear is very closely related to the immediate non-verbal context. I have argued that, at the outset of development, children exploit this relationship in order to discover how words are used and I showed in the last chapter that children's own initial uses of words are very closely modelled on frequently occurring adult uses.

In order for a hearing child to observe relationships between spoken words and the immediate context it is not, of course, necessary for the child to be looking at the speaker—and, much of the time, a child's visual attention will be directed towards objects and activities rather than the speaker. However, the attentional requirements for learning sign language are very different (as, indeed, are those for a deaf child learning an oral language). Perceiving sign language requires visual attention to the hands and face of the signer. (Looking at the hands is not enough because important information is also conveyed through facial expression.) And so, for the young deaf child to observe relationships between a sign and its immediate context, it might be necessary to divide attention between the language that is being presented and the context in which that language is occurring. At its most extreme, this could lead to a situation in which a child actually has to stop attending to an activity or object in order to attend to the adult signing that describes that activity or object, and the results of Study 2 (reported in Chapter 5) suggest that this could have a potentially deleterious effect on early language development, since a slight asynchrony in timing can have a large effect upon a child's language experience.

Studies have shown that the requirement for visual attention often leads to communication difficulties between deaf children and their hearing parents, which may still be present by the time the child enters school (Swisher, 1986; Wood et al., 1986). Other studies have suggested that, by contrast, deaf children from deaf families adapt to this requirement with relative ease, and recent studies of ASL development in children growing up in a signing environment have reported a rate of development that is comparable to spoken language (Caselli, 1983, 1987; Petitto, 1988; Volterra, 1981; Volterra & Caselli, 1985). There is also evidence that, when children first use signs, they do so to refer to objects, individuals and events within the immediate context, just as hearing children initially use words (Folven, Bonvillian & Orlansky, 1984/5).

It would appear, then, that the potentially difficult attentional problem that I described earlier does not, in practice, pose a problem for the child learning to sign in a signing home. However, if this is the case, a number of questions spring to mind. First, how do deaf children learn about the relationship between a sign and its context, and how is the attentional problem solved? Secondly, are there differences among children in the opportunities that are afforded for acquiring knowledge of such relationships? And, if there are differences, does this affect the rate at which children build up a sign vocabulary? A preliminary answer to these questions is provided by the study that I describe in the next section.

STUDY 4:
THE SOCIAL CONTEXT OF
EARLY SIGN LANGUAGE DEVELOPMENT

This study was carried out in collaboration with John Clibbens and has been reported in detail in Harris, Clibbens, Chasin & Tibbitts (1989). It adopts the same general methodology as the three earlier studies in that a small group of children was observed at regular intervals and on each occasion a video-recording was made of the interaction that took place between mother and child.

Four children and their mothers took part in the study. All the mothers and children were profoundly deaf and, in the case of the children, deafness was diagnosed before the children were 3 months of age. (Children of deaf parents are routinely screened within a few weeks of birth for hearing loss as they are considered to be an "at risk" group.) The fathers were also all deaf and BSL was the main language used in the home.

Three of the children (one boy and two girls) were observed from the age of 7 months. The fourth child (a boy) took part in the study from the age of 15 months. Observation continued until the age of 2 years.

Data Collection

The children and their mothers were observed every month when a 20-min video-recording was made of free play. The majority of recordings were made in the laboratory but, since three of the children lived a considerable distance away, some recordings were made in the home and some in a school for the deaf where one of the mothers worked. As in the earlier studies with hearing children, the mothers were not told the precise purpose of the study, but they were aware that the researchers were interested in sign language development.

It was decided to concentrate analysis on four recording sessions made when the children were approximately 7, 10, 16 and 20 months of age. Information about the children's sign vocabulary at 24 months was also collected.

Analysis of the Interaction

The main purpose of the analysis was to reveal the relationship between maternal signing and the immediate non-verbal context. In the case of a hearing mother talking to a hearing child, it is possible to consider the relationship between language and context simply by considering each maternal utterance and determining whether or not it refers to an object or activity at the child's current focus of attention. In the case of sign language, however, the picture is complicated by the need to consider not only whether there is an immediate context for a maternal sign, but also whether the child can observe both the sign and the context simultaneously.

The starting point for the analysis was, therefore, to establish how many maternal utterances a child saw at each session and, having done that, to determine how many of these had a current context. Utterances with a current context that were visible to the child were then subjected to detailed analysis in order to find out what kind of strategies the mothers used when they were signing. The final stage was to assess the children's sign language development at 2 years and then to relate this to their signing experience.

Results

Maternal Signing

When, in Chapter 5, I described the varying relationship between maternal speech and its immediate non-verbal context I expressed the results as proportions. I did not say anything about the amount of language that the hearing children were exposed to in the recording sessions. Before revealing what emerged from the study of maternal signing, it is worth pointing out that the fewest number of spoken maternal utterances occurring in a 16-month observation session was 83 in 10 min. All analysis of maternal signing was based on 20 rather than 10 min of observation, so the comparable figure is actually 166 utterances.

Table 8.1 shows the total number of signed utterances produced by each of the deaf mothers at 7, 10, 16 and 20 months. It is clear from this table that the deaf children were being exposed to considerably fewer utterances than hearing children of a similar age. Another notable feature of maternal signing was that the majority of utterances consisted of a single sign. This is a characteristic that has also been reported by Woll and Kyle (1989) in their study of deaf infants born to deaf mothers.

The preponderance of single-sign utterances, however, contrasts sharply with the language experience of hearing children of the same

TABLE 8.1
Total Number of Signed Utterances Produced by the Mothers [a]

| Child | Age of child | | | |
	7 months	10 months	16 months	20 months
Ann	17 (17)	120 (111)	81 (63)	145 (114)
John	—	—	41 (41)	91 (88)
Elizabeth	0 (0)	42 (42)	13 (11)	44 (32)
Richard	21 (21)	117 (104)	101 (88)	97 (75)

[a] Total number of single-sign utterances is shown in brackets.

age. The average length of maternal utterances at 16 months to the hearing child I mentioned earlier was three words. Thus it would appear that the deaf children were not only being presented with fewer signed utterances than a hearing child but also with considerably fewer lexical items. And one child in the sample received a very small amount of signing: Even at 20 months, Elizabeth was presented with only 44 signed utterances of which 32 were single signs.

One reason why the amount of signing that the deaf children received was considerably less than the least amount of speech received by a hearing child stemmed from the requirements of visual attention. Table 8.3 shows that the majority of signed utterances were made by the mother while the child was looking at her. As one can see, the proportion of utterances seen by the child increased with age—suggesting that it gradually became easier for mothers to make signs visible—and by 16 months nearly 80% of maternal utterances were made when the child was looking. These data suggest that a deaf mother typically signs only when there is a good chance that her child will be able to see what she is signing. The hearing mother, of course, does not operate under the same constraint of visual attention, and so there are potentially many more opportunities to talk than to sign because a child does not have to look at the mother in order to hear what she is saying.

The deaf mothers also appeared to operate under another constraint in that analysis of the immediate non-verbal context of their signing revealed that a high proportion of signs were presented in such a way that both the signed utterance and its context could be seen simultaneously by the child. Table 8.2 shows the mean proportion of signs that were presented in the child's visual field, broken down into those that referred to an object or event at the child's current focus of attention (current context) and those that did not (potential context). The categorisation on the basis of context was carried out in exactly the same way as for the hearing children in the two studies described in Chapter 5. In this case, however, the critical proportion is that relating

TABLE 8.2

Mean Proportion of Signed Untterances Produced by the Mothers Within the
Child's Visual Field (cvf) Categorised According to Context

	Age of child			
	7 months	10 months	16 months	20 months
Current context	0.44	0.54	0.73	0.77
Potential context	0.00	0.07	0.04	0.03
Total presented within cvf	0.44	0.61	0.77	0.80

to utterances with a current context where the utterance itself is
presented in the child's visual field. This proportion is shown in the first
line of Table 8.2.

As I have already indicated, the proportion of maternal utterances
that was seen by the child increased with age. At 7 months, fewer than
half of the utterances occurred when the child was looking at the mother,
but this proportion increased steadily to the high figure of 80% at 20
months. What was remarkably constant, however, was that in the great
majority of cases where a child was able to observe what the mother was
signing, he/she was also able to observe the object or event to which the
signing related. At all ages, only a tiny proportion of signed utterances
that were seen by the child did not have a current context (see the second
line of Table 8.2).

At first sight, this might suggest that the language experience of the
deaf child learning sign language is identical to that of the hearing child
who is exposed to spoken language. However, although this was my first
reaction to the results of the analysis that are summarised in Table 8.2,
closer examination of the relationship between sign and context
revealed an unexpected level of complexity, which made a direct
comparison of the deaf and hearing child more difficult than it first
appeared.

Individual Differences in Maternal Signing Strategies
Given that deaf mothers appear to be very good at presenting signs in
such a way that both the sign and its immediate non-verbal context are
available to the child, it seemed relevant to analyse maternal signing in
more detail in order to discover how this visual meshing of sign and
context was achieved.

There are essentially two ways in which a mother can ensure that
her child can see what she is signing while focusing attention on the
object or activity on which she is commenting. The first strategy is for
the mother to note what object or activity is engaging the child's

attention and then to sign in such a way that the child can see what she is signing without having to change his/her focus of attention. The second strategy is for the mother to change the child's focus of attention so that he/she is looking in the right place to see what is signed.

This distinction is related, although not identical to, the notion of child-initiated *vs* mother-initiated episodes. The second strategy is mother-initiated: the mother directs the child's attention in order to introduce language. The first strategy can be either child-initiated or mother-initiated depending on what factors determined the child's pre-existing focus of attention: if the mother takes her cue from the child's activity then her use of signing is child-initiated; if, on the other hand, she directs the child's activity, then her signing is mother-initiated.

What was particularly striking about the language of the hearing mothers described in the earlier studies was that it was set mainly in the context of child-initiated episodes. Hearing mothers most commonly began a new conversational topic in response to something done by the child; and once a topic was established, the most common pattern was that mother and child jointly engaged in the activity round which the mother's language was structured. This was true even for the mothers of the three slower developers in Study 2 (the problem there being not one of the child's level of participation in the interaction but one that arose either from the timing of maternal speech or the use of general rather than specific terms). The picture that emerged from analysis of the deaf mothers and children was, however, less homogeneous in this respect.

Since the pattern of interaction of each deaf mother and child was somewhat different, I will discuss each dyad in turn and explain which strategies each mother used in order to make both signs and their immediate context visible to the child. I will then go on to describe the sign language development of each of the children and to offer some speculations about how this might have been related to their language experience. In order to protect the identity the children and their mothers, the children have been given pseudonyms.

Ann

Table 8.3 shows the relative frequency of the different maternal signing strategies used by Ann's mother that enabled both a signed utterance and its immediate context to be visible. The two main strategies that I described above have been subdivided. The first strategy—signing within the child's pre-existing focus of attention—has two subdivisions based on the location of the mother's signing. Signs were either made in the normal location (usually in an area immediately in front of the

TABLE 8.3
Proportions of Different Signing Strategies Used by Ann's Mother

| | Age of child | | |
Mother's Strategy	7–10 months	16 months	20 months
Signs within child's pre-existing focus of attention			
in normal location	0.27	0.22	**0.65**
in displaced location			
on/in front of C	**0.67**	0.09	0.00
in C's visual field	0.04	**0.62**	0.25
Manipulates child's attention immediately before signing	0.02	0.07	0.10

Note: Most frequently used strategy at each age is shown in **bold**.

signer's body—the signing space) or they were physically displaced. This displacement could also be subdivided. Signs were either made in front of or on the child's own body—in the child's signing space—or they were displaced so that they were visible to the child but were not in the signing space of either mother or child.

As Table 8.3 shows, Ann's mother adapted her strategy as her daughter became older. At the 7- and 10-month sessions her most common strategy was to displace her signs onto or immediately in front of Ann, often placing her hands between the child and the object of Ann's attention. By 16 months, her strategy had changed and she most commonly displaced her signs into Ann's visual field. At this stage, signs were often not made close to Ann, but they could still usually be seen without Ann having to turn her head.

At 20 months, another change was apparent. As in all earlier sessions, Ann's mother most commonly signed at her daughter's pre-existing focus of attention. But she now most commonly signed in normal location, that is, in her own signing space: she displaced only a small proportion of her signs.

The data in Table 8.3 refer only to signed utterances where the child could see both sign and context. So one may wonder how it was possible that, at 20 months, Ann could see signs that her mother made in normal location and at the same time be focusing attention on the object or activity that her mother was describing. The explanation is that, by 20 months, Ann was turning to look up at her mother and then turning back to resume her activity. She was thus able to see what her mother was signing while keeping in mind what it was that was currently occupying her attention.

The most significant point about the strategies that Ann's mother adopted at each age was that they served to bring language into a pre-existing context of the child's activity. Initially, she physically displaced signs to bring them into Ann's focus of attention. Later, when Ann had learned to look up at her mother, her signs could have a current context without needing to be physically displaced. The use of age-appropriate strategies meant that the quality of Ann's language experience was very similar to that of a hearing child. For her, maternal language was related to objects and activities on which she was focusing attention.

The quantity of Ann's sign language experience was, however, different from that of a hearing child: Just because the amount of signing to which Ann was exposed was significantly less than the amount of spoken language presented to a hearing child of the same age, there were relatively fewer opportunities for Ann to relate language to a familiar non-verbal context. And, as I will shortly argue, I think this had an effect on the speed with which Ann acquired signs.

John

The pattern of signing by John's mother was superficially very similar to that of Ann's mother. We only had data on maternal signing at 16 and 20 months, but this showed that John's mother changed from signing in the child's visual field at the earlier session to signing in normal location at the later session (see Table 8.4). However, there was one significant difference between maternal signing at 20 months for John and Ann. At 20 months, Ann was turning to look at her mother so that she was able to observe signs made in normal location. However, at the same age, John had not learned to look towards his mother in order to check

TABLE 8.4
Proportions of Different Signing Strategies Used by John's Mother

Mother's Strategy	Age of child	
	16 months	20 months
Signs within child's pre-existing focus of attention		
in normal location	0.34	**0.60**
in displaced location		
on/in front of C	0.00	0.03
in C's visual field	**0.60**	0.15
Manipulates child's attention immediately before signing	0.06	0.22

Note: Most frequently used strategy at each age is shown in **bold**.

whether she was signing. Thus, when his mother signed in normal location, he frequently did not see an entire sign and it seemed very unlikely that he was taking in enough information to be able to note its defining characteristics.

One clear indication of the difference in the looking patterns of John and Ann was that the average length of John's glances toward his mother at 20 months was less than 1 sec and his total amount of looking in 20 min was 26 sec. The average length of Ann's glances at the same age was nearly 3 sec and she spent 114 sec looking at her mother (see Harris et al., 1989, for a detailed discussion of the looking patterns of the four children).

Elizabeth

The signing strategies of Elizabeth's mother were also very similar to those of Ann's mother as Table 8.5 shows. Her most common strategy was initially to sign in her daughter's signing space. But by 16 months, she had begun to sign in normal location on the majority of occasions. Elizabeth's visual attention to her mother was not as prolonged as that of Ann but, at 20 months, the average length of her glances was nearly 2 sec and considerably longer than John's.

However, if one refers back to Table 8.1, one will see that Elizabeth was presented with considerably less signing than any of the other children. Thus, although she had good opportunities to observe signs being used in context, she had relatively fewer opportunities than Ann. Accordingly, it might expected that her language development would be slower than Ann's but faster than that shown by John who, at 20 months, was giving only the most cursory of glances towards his mother's signs.

TABLE 8.5

Proportions of Different Signing Strategies Used by Elizabeth's Mother

Mother's Strategy	Age of child		
	7–10 months	*16 months*	*20 months*
Signs within child's pre-existing focus of attention			
in normal location	0.24	**0.73**	**0.77**
in displaced location			
on/in front of C	**0.43**	0.00	0.00
in C's visual field	0.14	0.18	0.15
Manipulates child's attention immediately before signing	0.19	0.09	0.08

Note: Most frequently used strategy at each age is shown in **bold**.

Richard

The signing strategies used by the mothers of Ann, John and Elizabeth were remarkably similar. All three initially displaced signs in a way that made them visible to the child and later they began signing in normal location. The pattern shown by Richard's mother was different in that she was remarkably consistent in her use of strategies throughout the observation period. Table 8.4 shows that, at all ages, her most common strategy was to sign within the child's pre-existing focus of attention but in normal location.

Now I have just explained that signing in normal location was a strategy that was appropriate for Ann and Elizabeth at 20 months (because they had learned to look up at their mothers), but it was less appropriate for John who gave his mother only the briefest of glances. At 20 months, Richard spent about the same amount of time looking at his mother as Elizabeth did, so there was no obvious reason why signing in normal location should not have been an appropriate strategy. However, as it turned out, the use of this strategy from the age of 7 months onwards presented Richard with some problems.

Richard's mother was able to sign in normal location even during the first year of his life because of a significant difference between the way that she used language and the way that the other three mothers did. Whereas the language used by the first three mothers was typically a comment upon their children's activity, Richard's mother adopted a more directive style. Her most common strategy was to direct Richard's attention towards herself—often by taking hold of an object that Richard had shown interest in and holding it up—and then to sign. She was able to sign in normal location because she directed his attention towards

TABLE 8.6
Proportions of Different Signing Strategies Used by Richard's Mother

Mother's Strategy	Age of child		
	7–10 months	*16 months*	*20 months*
Signs within child's pre-existing focus of attention			
in normal location	**0.56**	**0.70**	**0.66**
in displaced location			
on/in front of C	0.03	0.00	0.03
in C's visual field	0.13	0.18	0.18
Manipulates child's attention immediately before signing	0.28	0.12	0.13

Note: Most frequently used strategy at each age is shown in **bold**.

herself before signing. Her signs were thus usually made within Richard's pre-existing focus of attention since, before signing, she waited until his attention spontaneously moved towards her (because he was interested in the object that she picked up). However, she seldom signed when Richard was focusing attention upon an object or activity under his own control.

A study by Tomasello and Farrar (1986) suggests that language experience of this kind may not be conducive to the development of new vocabulary. In a study that was somewhat similar to Study 2, they examined the speech of mothers to children between the age of 15 and 21 months and found that individual differences in maternal references to current objects were positively correlated with the size of the children's vocabulary at 21 months. In other words, mothers who made a greater number of references to objects on which a child was currently focusing attention, had children with more precocious vocabulary development. However, there was a negative correlation between vocabulary size and a mother's use of object references that attempted to redirect the child's interest.

A similar pattern emerged from a teaching study carried out by the same authors. When adults attempted to teach new words to 17-month-old children, they were more successful when the words referred to objects on which the child was already focusing attention than they were when the child's attentional focus had to be redirected. What this might suggest, then, is that Richard's language experience, because it often involved redirecting his attention, would not provide an ideal context for acquiring signs.

Sign Language Development

At the outset, this study has not been concerned with rate of sign language development. The reason for this was that it was designed to discover what signing strategies deaf mothers used with their young children. I had not suspected that the four deaf mothers would show such different patterns and so had not anticipated that there might be developmental differences among the children in their sign development.

The relative sign language development of the four children thus had to be estimated from one of the recording sessions and, as in an earlier study, it was decided to sample language development at 2 years. Table 8.7 shows the number of different signs that each of the children produced in the 20 min of recording made at the observation session closest to their second birthday. The differences among the children were dramatic. Ann produced 16 different signs, Elizabeth produced 7, Richard produced only 1 and John did not produce any.

TABLE 8.7
Signs Produced at 24-month Observation Session by the Four Children

Child	Signs				
Ann	HURT	FISH	PLEASE	COW	WHERE
	SLEEP	RED	COAT	BOAT	RABBIT
	THANK-YOU	BREAK	BLACK	HEAD	CRY
	NO				
John	none				
Elizabeth	BUILD-UP	WHAT	DOG	CAT	WHERE
	BIG	MINE			
Richard	BABY				

These estimates of relative signing ability were almost certainly accurate, since at each observation session we had asked whether any new signs had been produced. At 24 months, Ann's mother reported that her child was using a large number of different signs. The mothers of John and Richard both thought that their sons were not yet signing and Elizabeth's mother reported the appearance of a few signs.

The language development of the four children can best be set in context by comparing it with that of the hearing children in Study 2, whose vocabulary development at 2 years was also sampled. In the case of the hearing children, the estimate of relative vocabulary size was derived from a 10-min sample, rather than a 20-min sample, but even so the slowest of the normal developers still produced 20 different words (in comparison to the 16 signs produced by Ann) and the most precocious hearing child produced 77 different words. The slower developers in Study 2 used between 9 and 14 different words and Ann's development would appear to be more in line with this.

Language Experience and Early Sign Language Development

As we have just seen, there was considerable variation in the number of signs that the four deaf children could produce by the age of 2 years. Two of the children appeared to be very delayed in their language production, but even the two faster developers knew fewer lexical items than a hearing child of the same age. I want to suggest that these differences among the deaf children, and the differences between the deaf children and hearing children, arose from differences in language experience. Such suggestions are necessarily only speculative because the sample is small, but they should be seen within the wider context of the arguments that I have made in the earlier chapters.

Ann, the child who knew most signs at 2 years, had language experience that was most similar to that of a hearing child. Her mother signed about objects and activities that were at Ann's focus of attention and, like a hearing mother, she frequently used language to comment upon child-initiated activities. The total amount of sign language to which Ann was exposed was, however, considerably less than the amount of spoken language presented to a hearing child, and this was almost certainly a direct result of the logistic difficulties of presenting a sign in such a way that both it and its immediate context could be seen. Significantly, the amount of signing used by Ann's mother increased considerably from 16 to 20 months, when she no longer had to displace signs, and it continued to increase in later sessions. This indicates that, once Ann's mother was able to sign in normal location because she could rely on her daughter looking at her, she was able to introduce much more language into her interaction with Ann. However, for at least the first 16 months of life, in comparison to most hearing children, Ann had been presented with relatively few opportunities to relate signs to a familiar context, and this is almost certainly why her early lexical development was also slower than that of most hearing children.

A more extreme effect of quantity of language experience can be seen in the sign production of Elizabeth whose mother produced the smallest number of signed utterances. In the 20-month session, Elizabeth was presented with only two signed utterances per minute—compared with over seven for Ann—and most of these were single signs: at 2 years Elizabeth was producing considerably fewer signs than Ann.

Elizabeth's progress was, however, considerably faster than that of John and Richard, neither of whom had begun to establish a sign vocabulary at 2 years. In both cases, I think that this slow lexical development was the result of impoverished language experience. In John's case, the problem seems to have been that his mother began signing in normal location before he had learned to break off from his activity in order to look up at her. Richard's problem is more difficult to characterise, but it appeared to stem from the fact that his language experience was not rooted in activity that he had initiated. Indeed, one of the most noticeable effects of Richard's language experience was to make him generally reluctant to communicate with his mother. For him, language was not something that grew naturally out of developing patterns of interaction; indeed, it was something that often disrupted the interaction with his mother because she tended to break into an activity, take away the toy that Richard was playing with, and then label it.

If you have followed my argument so far, you may have concluded that providing a deaf child with enough of the right kind of early language experience is a potentially difficult task. You might then wonder why, as I noted earlier, studies of sign language development report that children reach various language "milestones" at about the same age as children who are acquiring a spoken language. For example, Caselli (1987) claims that two-sign combinations occur at around the same age as two-word combinations.

I do not want to dispute claims about the development of sign combinations, since they appear reasonably convincing. However, what is relevant to my argument is what typically occurs with early sign vocabulary development. The picture here is unclear for two reasons. First, many studies have not drawn a systematic distinction between signs, gestures and other hand movements (for a discussion of this problem, see Petitto, 1988; Woll & Kyle, 1989). As we saw in Chapter 7, identifying early words is by no means a simple task and, if anything, identifying early signs is even more difficult. The second area of concern arises from the samples of children whose sign language development has been recorded. Some have been the hearing children of deaf parents (and so do not have the same problem of needing to rely heavily on visual cues to direct their attention to signing), and many of the other children studied have had highly educated parents. Relatively little is known about the range of vocabulary development that occurs within the whole population of deaf children born to deaf parents, and it remains a possibility that the processes determining the mastery of early vocabulary may be different from those controlling the emergence of two-word combinations in children's speech. Some evidence in favour of this view comes from recent research into the language development of children who are born blind and I begin the final chapter with a brief discussion of these findings.

Language Experience and Early Language Development

LANGUAGE DEVELOPMENT IN BLIND CHILDREN

In the last few years there has been a renewed interest in the early language development of blind children. This has stemmed from a feeling among some child language researchers that comparing the language development of blind children with that of sighted children provides a test case for determining how much of development is the product of experience and how much the result of innately determined processes. The rationale for this belief is that a blind child, with no other handicaps, will have the same innate endowment as a sighted child but very different experience. Thus, if language development is dependent upon language experience, the language development of blind and sighted children should be substantially different. If, on the other hand, language development is mainly determined by innate endowment, it should be substantially similar for the two groups. As one might expect, it turns out that this is a false dichotomy.

Early Social Development

Given what I have argued about the importance of early social experience, it is interesting to note that, in many respects, the development of blind and sighted children is similar. Early on, blind infants smile at the sound of their parents' voices (Freedman, 1964) and, at around 8 months, they become anxious at the sound of unfamiliar voices (Fraiberg, Siegal & Gibson, 1966). Sitting, standing and supported walking also follow the same time course as for sighted babies, although some aspects of motor development—rolling over, getting up into a sitting position, pulling up to standing and walking—do appear to be delayed.

Lewis (1987) suggests that blind infants find self-initiated changes in movement particularly difficult. Part of the reason for this is that there are few incentives for the blind child to change position: Sighted children are always trying to reach out to objects and changes in position often arise because the child wants to be able to see something better or to reach for it. Reaching is also delayed and blind babies typically do not reach out for a toy until 10–11 months, several months after most sighted babies (Fraiberg, 1977; Bower, 1974; Bigelow, 1983).

These bare statistics do not, however, reflect the essential difference between the early social world of the blind and sighted child. As we saw in Chapter 3, the sighted infant becomes increasingly able to share in the perceptual experience of the adult. Babies become increasingly sophisticated, both at identifying which object another person is looking at, and also at producing and understanding pointing. Such opportunities are not open to the blind baby and this appears to have some important consequences for early language development.

Vocabulary Development

The most extensive studies of blind children's vocabulary development have been carried by Landau and Gleitman (1985) and Dunlea (1989). The conclusions these authors draw from their studies are somewhat different and can be seen as a reflection of contrasting views about the role of language experience. However, close inspection of their findings reveals a rather more consistent picture.

The study by Landau and Gleitman followed the language development of two children—Kelli and Carlo—who were blind from birth. Both children took a long time to say their first word: Kelli was 23 months old and Carlo 26 months. Landau and Gleitman conclude that "relatively late onset of speech is characteristic for blind children" (p.27). However, they place considerable emphasis on the fact that, although lexical development is delayed, the semantic categories used by the blind children were identical to those of sighted children. According to Landau and Gleitman, "blind children talk about what most young children talk about: mommies, daddies, dolls, cookies and toys" (p.30), and they conclude from this that, despite experiential differences, the conceptual underpinnings of early lexical development are identical for blind and sighted children.

As an example of the conceptual similarity of the lexicon of the blind and sighted child, Landau and Gleitman describe a series of experiments that tested Kelli's understanding of the verbs "look" and "touch". These showed that, when asked to "look" at an object, Kelli would explore it with her hands. But when asked to "touch but not look", Kelli touched, banged or stroked an object, but did not manually explore it. The conclusion that Landau and Gleitman draw from these findings is that there is a common basis for the meaning ascribed to "look" by blind and sighted children. For the sighted child, "looking" involves exploration with the eyes. For the blind child, "looking" also involves exploring with the dominant modality used for object perception, in this case, touch.

Another example of a blind child's understanding of a sighted verb comes from Mills (1987). She describes Lisa as using "see" with respect to the auditory modality. Having complained that she could not "see" the noise being made by a tape-recorder, Lisa moved into a better position to hear it. This example is similar to Kelli's interpretation of "look" in that it involves the substitution of a modality that is salient to a blind child for one that is not. It suggests, however, that the modality chosen by a blind child as an alternative to that of vision may vary from child to child.

Dunlea (1989) also concludes that blind children utilise haptic-kinaesthetic information in lieu of visual information but she sees the lack of visual information as having much more extensive consequences. She presents a detailed account of the acquisition of the first 100 words by three blind children and, unlike Landau and Gleitman, she sets this against the background of earlier studies that have considered the social context of early language experience. Although the blind child can hear what is being said, opportunities for observing the social context in which words occur are severely limited. Dunlea's study shows that this restriction has some important implications for early language development. For, although the blind children acquired new words at roughly the same rate as sighted children, they did not show the same pattern of development. In comparison to sighted children, the blind children's use of words was rigid: They were generally very unwilling to extend their initial use of words either beyond the scope of their own action or to unfamiliar objects. This makes them very different from sighted children who, as we saw in Chapter 7, very rapidly extend their use of individual words. Indeed, one of the most striking features of sighted children's early lexical development is that many words are used in a contextually flexible way right from the outset. Another feature of the lexical development of the blind children studied by Dunlea was that they showed a very steady rate of vocabulary development. There was no sign of the typical burst in rate of acquisition that occurs after the first 30 or so words.

As we saw in Chapter 6, the initial period of early vocabulary development has been characterised as one in which children learn that words are used to refer to objects and events in the world. Dunlea's contention is that, even by the end of the single-word period, blind children have not yet learned this. She argues that visual experience has an important role in guiding the development of the conceptual processes that underpin lexical development in the single-word period.

Early Syntactic Development

Dunlea's data also suggest that, in one important sense, early syntactic development occurs independently of lexical development. She found that, despite differences in the early lexicon, the blind children progressed to multi-word utterances at much the same point as sighted children. Once they had a vocabulary of around 100 words, they began to produce combinations even though, at this stage, much of their lexical knowledge was still highly restricted. Dunlea concludes that, for the blind child, the stimulus to begin combining words appears to be independent of their state of lexical knowledge.

The study by Landau and Gleitman can also be seen as compatible with the view that, despite some initial delay in vocabulary development, blind children show a normal rate of syntactic development. They found that by 36 months their blind subjects had reached the same stage of language development as sighted children. This prompts the thought that, although the initial phase of lexical development appears to be influenced by experience, there may be a universal ontogenetic progression in early syntactic development.

THE ROLE OF EXPERIENCE IN LANGUAGE DEVELOPMENT
What Language Experience Does

By now you will have realised that a consistent pattern is beginning to emerge from the various studies that I have described. They all point to the fact that the child's early experience has an important role to play in early lexical development but a much lesser role in syntactic development. What I want to do in the final sections of this book is to examine in more detail the theoretical implications of this claim. The evidence from Dunlea's study is particularly illuminating because it shows that any explanation of the role of experience in lexical development must involve an account of the role of perceptual as well as linguistic experience. I will begin by summarising the evidence concerning linguistic experience, since it is this that has been addressed so far. I will then go on to discuss the limitations of linguistic experience and its interrelation with perceptual experience.

What I have argued so far is that studies of the relationship between adult speech to children and language development have shown the influence of adult speech to be very specific. In Chapter 2, I reviewed some of the recent studies of adult speech to children and concluded that, although there was good evidence that certain aspects of morpho-syntactic development—notably the development of auxiliaries—were related to very specific aspects of adult speech, there appeared to be no simple relationship between the syntactic complexity of adult speech and the rate of syntactic development. However, a rather different picture emerges in the case of lexical development. There it would appear, from the results of studies described in Chapters 5 and 7, that the child's language experience has a very direct influence on the way that early word meanings develop. Children's first uses of words are strikingly similar to the most frequent maternal use of these same words, although subsequent uses of these first words are much less grounded in maternal use.

I have also argued that the speed of early lexical development is influenced by the extent to which adult speech affords the child with opportunities to note systematic patterns of relationship between heard words and observed context. In Chapter 5, I described a study in which the language experience of three children with slow language development was compared to that of a group of faster developers. The comparison revealed that the language experience of the former group afforded considerably fewer opportunities to note the contemporaneous occurrence of familiar contexts and often repeated words. I also described a study of young deaf children learning sign language (see Chapter 8) that suggests that being able to relate an adult word to a familiar context is a vital aspect of early word learning, which can be made much more difficult if adult language presents the child with few opportunities to note such relationships.

It is worth underlining this last point if only because it is probably the most controversial of my claims. Few would deny that the early lexicon is more or less rooted in experience, but what may be difficult to accept is that the *quantity* as well as the quality of the child's experience appears to be important. For it could, in theory, be the case that all the child requires is a single observation of some pairing between a word and a context. However, there are several reasons for believing that this is not the case at the outset of lexical development.

I discussed some of the evidence concerning frequency in Chapter 7, where I described our study of the relationship between maternal speech and early lexical development: For the great majority of words that the child acquired, initial use mirrored the mother's most frequent use. Data from an experimental study by Gunzi (unpublished) also supported this view, since she found that the frequency with which novel object names were presented to three infants had a significant effect on their acquisition.

Before concluding this section, it is interesting to note the findings of three other studies that highlight the significance of frequency. The first, by Schwartz and Terrell (1983), was an experimental study in which the frequency with which words were presented was strictly controlled. The study showed that frequency of presentation had an influence on acquisition. Furrow and Nelson (1984) report data from an observational study which compared the language experience of children whose early speech was classified as either referential or expressive (using the original distinction characterised by Nelson, 1973). Mothers of expressive children (who have a high proportion of personal-social words in their early vocabulary) made proportionally more person references than mothers of referential children. In contrast, mothers of referential children (who have a high proportion of object names) made more references to objects.

The final study that deserves a mention is that of Budwig and Wiley (1991), since their data not only support the view that the relative frequency of word use by mothers has an important influence upon the early stages of word use by their children, but they also point to that fact that such influences rapidly fall away. The Budwig and Wiley study is of children's early self-reference where they found interesting individual differences. Some children used "I" to refer to themselves, whereas others used "me". When the mothers' own uses of these words were examined, there proved to be a close relationship between maternal style and the child's own choice of word: Mothers who most often used "I" had children who also used "I", whereas mothers who tended to use "me" had children who used the "me" form. However, when the children began to expand their forms of self-reference, the close link between maternal use and child use disappeared. This finding is strikingly similar to the data presented in Chapter 7 concerning the existence or otherwise of maternal precedents for second uses of early words. There we saw that, in comparison to the very high proportion of first uses which mirrored one or more maternal uses, only a relatively small proportion of second uses were similarly modelled on the mother's use.

Is Early Experience Universal?

Having speculated about the role of language experience in early language development, I want to turn to a consideration of the limitations of experience. However, before addressing this question directly, I think that it is important to return to an issue that I raised briefly in Chapter 2. There I noted that it may be inappropriate to draw conclusions about universal aspects of language experience solely on the basis of studies of mother–child interaction in westernised cultures. Although there is not space in this book to consider such an issue in detail, I want to give a brief summary of some of the most relevant research on mother–child interaction in non-western cultures and then to consider its implications.

The first and best known studies in this area are those of Schieffelin and Ochs (1983) and Ochs and Schieffelin (1984). They report data on the Kaluli who live in the tropical rainforest of Papua New Guinea. The Kaluli live in extended family groups with two or more such groups living together, and as a result it is common for at least a dozen individuals of different ages to be living together in one house. This makes the early experience of Kaluli babies very different from that of children growing up in a nuclear family.

Everyday life among the Kaluli is overtly focused around talk which they think of and use as a means of control, manipulation, assertion and appeal as well as a means of expression. As Schieffelin and Ochs (1983) put it, "talk ... gets you want you want, need or feel owed" and so Kaluli parents see learning how to talk as a major goal of socialisation.

Kaluli mothers are attentive to their infants and rarely leave them alone. Up to the age of 6 months, when not holding them, mothers carry their babies in netted bags which are suspended from their heads. Babies are offered the breast whenever they cry but, while nursing her baby, a mother may also be engaged in some other activity such as preparing food or talking to another member of the household. In marked contrast to middle-class western mothers, Kaluli mothers never treat their babies as communicative partners. Since they believe that infants "have no understanding", Kaluli mothers rarely talk to their babies other than to greet them by name. Even more strikingly, they do not gaze into their infants' eyes and, rather than holding their babies facing towards them, Kaluli mothers tend to face their babies outwards so that they are part of the wider social group.

Another way in which the early social experience of Kaluli and western babies is dramatically different is evident when older children talk to the baby. (Presumably other adults do not attempt to talk to the baby for the same reason that the mother does not.) The mother replies to the older child using a special nasal, high-pitched voice that indicates she is talking on behalf of her baby. She speaks assertively, using language that is well-formed and appropriate for an older child. These exchanges seem designed primarily for the older child and they have no origin in any action or vocalisation made by the infant.

Contrast this with the very child-centred pattern of mothers' speech that I described in Chapter 5. Even when western babies are only a few months old, their mothers treat their actions and vocalisations as though they have intention. Western babies are treated as conversational partners from the first months of life, which is why, even at 6 months of age, it is possible for two-thirds of conversational exchanges to be child-initiated (see Table 5.3). Among the Kaluli, however, a very different attitude prevails. It is a central part of Kaluli cultural belief that no person can know what someone else—even another adult—is feeling or thinking. In this context, it makes no sense for a Kaluli mother to attempt an interpretation of her baby's intentions.

When Kaluli babies start to babble, this makes little difference to adult expectations. In marked contrast to views that prevail among many western parents, babbling is not regarded as communicative nor as related to the speech that will be produced later. Occasionally, adults or older children may repeat a baby's vocalisation, making it into the name of someone in the household, but they do not expect the baby to imitate them nor do they treat the original vocalisation as an attempt to produce a real word.

From 6 months onwards, Kaluli babies also receive a limited set of imperatives and rhetorical questions as well as greetings. For example, when a child attempts to take an object that belongs to someone else, an adult might ask "Is it yours?!" or "Who are you?!", the object being in both cases to "shame" the child. Other than this limited range of utterances, however, very little talk is directed to the young child.

This does not, however, mean that young Kaluli children are brought up in an impoverished linguistic environment. Although relatively little speech is directed *to* the child, the verbal environment surrounding young children is rich and varied. Given that the infant spends all day with members of the extended family, there is much speech to overhear. Presumably, much of this will relate to actions and objects that the child can observe and, as the child grows older and begins to engage in a greater range of activities, members of the household—especially older children—will often comment upon these, using the child's name. They will say things like "Look at Seligiwo! He's walking."

It is clear from the description provided by Schieffelin and Ochs that Kaluli and western children receive very different language experience in the period before they begin to use identifiable words. Their experience continues to be different once the first words appear—specifically the words for "breast" and "mother"—because Kaluli mothers then use an explicit teaching strategy in which they model appropriate utterances for the child. Each utterance is followed by the word "ɛlɛma", which means "say like that". Mothers use this method of direct instruction in order to teach the children to use assertive language. They also correct the phonology, morphology and lexical form of their children's utterances as well as semantic and pragmatic content. Kaluli mothers do not, however, expand or elaborate their children's utterances —because of their view that it is impossible to know what another person is thinking or intending—and they do not label objects.

The many differences between the language experience of Kaluli and western children show that the model of the mother adapting her language to her child is by no means universal. However, what is of interest for the purpose of the present discussion is whether the kind of language that Kaluli children hear has an effect on their rate of language development. What might we predict?

One problem in interpreting the observations of Schieffelin and Ochs—and in making predictions about the language development of Kaluli children—is that these authors do not quantify the amount and variety of language that the children can observe. Furthermore, there is little detailed information about the language development of individual children. It is clear from what they report that Kaluli children are exposed to a great deal of language that relates to current activity among various members of the extended family and some speech actually describes the children's own activities. So one might predict that Kaluli infants have sufficient linguistic experience of the right kind to enable them to begin producing words. However, one might also predict that the lack of object naming, on the one hand, and the frequent repetition of formulistic phrases, on the other, might lead to a pattern of language development that is initially rather different from that of western children. Data from Schieffelin and Ochs (1983) show that Kaluli children in the second year of life are very good at repeating phrases when directed to do so by their mothers. What we do not know, however, is how good they are at producing language spontaneously.

A study by Pye (1986) also lacks data on children's language development while providing a detailed account of adult speech. Pye's study is of the Mayan language Quiché, and he compares the speech used by Mayan parents with that used by parents in North America. One of his main findings was that Quiché mothers do not make significant prosodic adjustments when talking to their children and, unlike mothers in the United States, they do not use exaggerated intonation or speak more slowly. Most strikingly, Quiché mothers frequently reduce their voice so much that it becomes a whisper.

The general lack of prosodic modification is mirrored in a lack of syntactic modification. The Quiché mothers studied by Pye did not use shorter utterances when talking to their children, although they did appear to adopt a more fixed word order. Overall, there were few differences between speech to other adults and speech to children with morphological complexity, MLU and amount of repetition being similar.

Pye also reports that he did not see any Quiché mothers playing special games with their children. When asked whether they knew of any such games—nursery rhymes or games played with the fingers (such as "Incy wincy spider")—they said that they did not. This is consistent with Pye's claim that Quiché mothers wait until their children begin to talk before they converse with them. As in the case of the Kaluli, however, there is no reason to suppose that Quiché children are not surrounded by language.

The two studies that I have just described show very clearly that the way that adults talk to children is very dependent upon cultural expectations. Contrary to what we might suppose, the way that western mothers converse with their children in the first year of life is not universal. The fact that western mothers talk to children from the moment they are born stems from the view that the development of understanding begins at birth and, to a large extent, their style of baby talk is heavily influenced by the experience of observing other mothers.

A recent study of Japanese mothers also demonstrates the importance of cultural expectations. Todo, Fogel and Kawai (1990) report several differences between the speech of mothers from Japan and the United States when talking to their 3-month-old infants. Again beliefs and attitudes to child-rearing were important determinants of maternal speech style. Japanese mothers were more affect-oriented than US mothers, making more use of nonsense and onomatopoeic sounds and more frequently calling their baby by name. They also used grammatically complete utterances far less often. The US mothers were more information-oriented and directed and questioned their infants more often than Japanese mothers. There was, however, an interesting similarity between the two groups. Mothers in both countries talked most frequently about the actions of their infants (although the proportion was higher for US mothers than for Japanese).

As I have already suggested, these studies of motherese in other cultures raise interesting questions about the relationship between language experience and language development. Frustratingly, these are not questions that can be answered on the basis of current data. What is needed are cross-cultural studies that explore the relationship between verbal and non-verbal aspects of adult speech to children and early lexical and syntactic development. It is, however, possible to speculate. For what the studies of both Kaluli and Japanese mothers reveal is that much of the language that young children hear—be it addressed specifically to them or merely spoken in their presence—concerns the child's current world. And, while the prosodic and syntactic features of motherese may be culturally specific, it is likely that the content of the speech that children hear will have common features. If this proves to be so, we can ask two interesting questions: Given that these common features will be more or less evident in particular styles of motherese, is there a pattern of cross-cultural differences which mirrors those found within samples of western mothers, and do these cross-cultural differences give rise to analogous differences in language development?

What Language Experience Does Not Do

So far I have carefully avoided saying anything about the precise mechanism that underlies the development of the early lexicon other than to argue that the child is able to exploit a consistent relationship between a word and a familiar context. But this is not an issue that I can continue to ignore.

To say that the young child arrives at the use—and meaning—of early words by noting a consistent correspondence between a word used by an adult and a familiar non-verbal context could imply various things. One possible interpretation of this claim is that it is, in essence, a behaviourist account. According to such an account, the child hears a word used in a particular situation on a number of occasions and then learns to reproduce that word when an identical situation recurs. According to an account of this kind, the child is merely responding in a stimulus-bound fashion when saying a word and is behaving in exactly the way that Skinner described in his account of lexical acquisition (see Chapter 1). This is the interpretation that is outlined by Ninio (1992) when she says that our data concerning the relationship between first words and maternal speech imply that the child is responding in some holistic fashion to "a complete, unanalysed physical and behavioural situation".

I find this ascription somewhat surprising because, if anything, the view that has been implicit in earlier discussions of these issues (see, for example, Harris et al., 1986, 1988) has been what Stemmer (1989) describes as a "cognitivist view". This kind of view says that in the period before acquiring his/her first words, the child builds up certain non-linguistic representations. The child then consistently hears the adult using a particular word at the same time that the child has an active mental representation of some aspect or aspects of the context. The child learns the meaning of a word by matching the two together and attaching the word to the pre-existing representation. This is the view that is presented in the Ellis and Wells (1980) paper that I discussed in Chapter 2. There the authors note, in their discussion of the frequent use of imperatives by the parents of children with precocious language development, that:

> ... parental commands may strongly aid development of the system of symbolic representation by encoding just those relations to which the child is attending and which he has already represented to himself enactively and/or iconically (Ellis & Wells, 1980, p.56).

This view begs a number of questions. In essence, these all stem from a single problem which was originally set out by Quine (1960). Quine's concern was with the difficulties of a linguist in an alien world but many people have seen this as an analogy for the problems encountered by the child learning language. There is, however, likely to be an important difference between the case of the linguist and that of the child in that the latter will often encounter words in a situation where the speaker is aware of potential problems of incomprehension and will attempt to provide some non-verbal support for his/her utterance (see Zukow, 1990, for a discussion of the various cues to meaning potentially available to the child).

Quine's particular example concerns the situation where someone hears the word "gavagai!" while a rabbit runs by, but as I am more interested in cats—as are almost all of the young children I have ever studied—I will illustrate the problem with a cat example. Imagine that a child hears the word "cat" and, at the same time, observes a cat sitting on the window sill. The child's attention is drawn to the cat by the speaker—perhaps by pointing or by gaze. How does the child work out what is the referential scope of "cat"? The non-verbal context will have narrowed down some of the possibilities but many remain: The particular cat (that is, the cat's personal name), the particular cat sitting down, the particular cat sitting on a/the window sill, cats in general, cats (in general) sitting down, cats (in general) sitting on a/the window sill, small furry animate beings (with tails), a tail, the act of sitting or the act of sitting on a window sill ...

Markman and Hutchinson (1984), who obviously prefer dogs to cats, describe the problem as follows:

> Young children beginning to acquire their native language continually face this problem of narrowing down the meaning of a term from an

indefinite number of possibilities. Someone points in some direction and then utters a word. On what grounds is the child to conclude that a new unfamiliar word, e.g. "dog", refers to dogs? (Markman & Hutchinson, 1984, p.2).

However, as Landau and Gleitman (1985) point out, the potential ambiguity of reference is even greater than the original example given by Quine suggests. Children sometimes—perhaps often—have *false experiences* where they are observing one thing and the adult says something that is quite unrelated. For example, a child may be playing with toys when the adult says "It's time for your bath". Another problem noted by Landau and Gleitman is that of *abstract meanings*. They point out that many words learned by children at a relatively young age have no direct sensory-perceptual correlates. A final problem that can be added to this list is that of *language specificity*. Comparisons among even closely related languages reveal that the relationship between words and concepts is not invariant—distinctions that are made in one language may not be made in another (see Durrell, 1988, for a discussion of this issue with respect to German and English).

The claim that children are initially very reliant on frequent pairing between word and context explains how the problem of false experiences can be overcome. The problem of abstract meaning is a much less tractable one, but it is relevant to note that such meanings are the product of the third phase of vocabulary development rather than the two earlier phases. However, the essential problem posed by Quine remains and one solution has been to posit the existence of innate constraints on the kinds of concept that the child attaches to a lexical item.

It should be noted that there is an inherent problem with the notion of innate constraints just because word–concept relationships are by no means universal. However, before worrying about that, it is important to clarify exactly what is meant by the term "constraint". In particular, it is important to be able to distinguish a constraint from a bias or preference that children might show in their lexical development.

WHAT ABOUT INNATE CONSTRAINTS?

Are there Innate Constraints on Development?

Nelson (1988) describes four characteristics of constraints, although she notes that most researchers do not admit them all. The characteristics are: *language specificity* (constraints are not perceptual but are triggered by language-specific processes); *species specificity* (constraints are not shown by infra-human species); *innateness* (constraints are universal and invariant). The fourth characteristic is that constraints *do not show developmental change.*

There are obviously problems in demonstrating the existence of the last two properties of constraints. A process may be innate but not necessarily invariant except at a high level of abstraction; and it may be innate but also maturational (in which case it will show developmental change). It is also the case that universality is not necessarily evidence of innateness, and also true that a process can appear to vary because of some other process with which it interacts. So, in practice, the arguments about innate constraints upon the development of the lexicon come down to two questions that are relatively tractable: Do children, but not chimpanzees, respect the distinction between objects and events when acquiring words, and do they respect distinctions within the object class?

We have already encountered some of the evidence about the distinction between object and event references in Chapter 1. There we saw that young children do sometimes violate the distinction between objects, properties and events. For example, Dromi (1986) found that early in development her daughter used the word "hot" both as a name for ovens and heaters and for the property of being either hot or cold. Dromi reports that, during the first 2 months of lexical production, most of her daughter's words were indeterminate in this way. We have found similar examples in a recent study (Harris, Yeeles, Chasin, & Oakley, in prep.). Ben used the word "bang" to describe a stone and also when he was banging the stone and other objects against something. He also used "see-saw" to describe both his see-saw and the action of rocking on the see-saw, and he used "bounce" both when he was bouncing up and down and also to refer to an inflatable car that he bounced on.

It is significant to note, however, that by no means all of the children in our sample produced what might be thought of as indeterminate uses of this kind and it is quite likely that this is an area of individual difference among children. It is, in any case, difficult to interpret apparently indeterminate uses. As we saw in Chapter 7, there are cases in the early stages of lexical development where a child appears to have acquired two distinct homonyms rather than a single word with a range of meanings. Also, it is hard to be sure exactly what a child is doing when using a word in several different ways. Hudson and Nelson (1984) have convincingly demonstrated that even very young children spontaneously use words in an analogical fashion, pointing to some functional similarity between the original referent and the novel one.

Some of the most compelling evidence for the view that children respect ontological categories comes from Huttenlocher and Smiley

(1987). They report that children's word use did not violate the distinction between objects, properties and events. The children studied by Huttenlocher and Smiley also applied object names to whole objects and did not use words to refer to specific object complexes such as object + particular action or object + particular location.

There are problems in interpreting these findings because of the methodology that Huttenlocher and Smiley adopted. One difficulty is that they identified the child's use of a word according to the *most common pattern* and thus would be unlikely to pick up cases of indeterminate use. Another is that they tested words on particular occasions using standard probes. They did not make use of diary records or extended observation and so may well have underestimated lexical development and only identified words at a relatively late stage of use. A final point to note is that, in their report of word use, Huttenlocher and Smiley relied mainly on data collected when the children were between 16 and 25 months of age. This covers a period that is typically several months after first word uses have appeared. The suggestion that the Huttenlocher and Smiley data are reflecting something other than the initial stage of lexical development is supported by the fact that the authors did not observe any changes in word use. As we saw in Chapter 7, changes in word use are very common at the outset of lexical development.

The final evidence that we should consider is that of Markman and Hutchinson (1984), which was described in Chapter 1 in the section on chimpanzee symbol use. It will be remembered that Markman and Hutchinson showed children a picture of an object which was given a nonsense name such as "dax". When asked to find "another dax that is the same as this dax", children chose another object from the same class as the original in preference to a related (thematic) picture from a different class. In a control condition, where the children were merely shown a picture but it was not given a label, far fewer children selected the object from the same class. As Nelson (1988) points out, these findings are problematic for two reasons. First, although the children chose an object from the same class as the original exemplar on a statistically significant number of occasions, their pattern of choice was by no means invariant. Just less than two-thirds of the choices were for the object from the same class which, as Nelson argues, could just as well be evidence for a preference or bias as for an innate constraint. The other problem, which was mentioned earlier in the context of the discussion of Kanzi the pygmy chimpanzee, was that the youngest children in the crucial experiment of the Markman and Hutchinson study had reached the grand old age of 4 years and were well past the early stages of learning to talk.

Bauer and Mandler (1987) adapted the methodology of the Markman and Hutchinson study for younger children, aged from 20 to 30 months. They found that younger children did not respond differentially in the labelling condition. Whether the first picture was labelled or not, the children showed a strong preference for objects from the same class. This finding suggests that the preference for thematic choices which Markman and Hutchinson found in the non-label condition is something that develops in the pre-school years and that there is a perceptually driven (i.e. non-linguistic) preference/constraint for grouping objects into taxonomic categories.

Language Experience and Innate Constraints

After that somewhat lengthy discussion of experimental studies of innate constraints, we are now in a position to be able to say something about the processes that occur in the early development of the lexicon. It is useful at this point to return to the findings from the Dunlea (1989) study, because these suggest that perceptual mechanisms have an important role to play in the establishment of the lexicon. What Dunlea showed was that the early lexical development of the blind children she studied differed from that of sighted children in two ways. First, the blind children continued to use words in a relatively context-bound way, that is, they carried on using a word in the same context as they had initially encountered it. Secondly, they acquired their first 100 words at a steady rate and did not show a typical vocabulary spurt.

For the sighted child, one of the most important aspects of early word learning that underpins much of the early contextually flexible usage, and also contributes to the vocabulary spurt, has to do with the realisation that objects have names. There are several, separable, aspects to this realisation: one is that there are such things as objects which have certain properties; another is that two people can refer to the same object; and another is that objects have names. The two former realisations would appear to be necessary for the latter.

To understand at least part of the reason why the blind child appears to struggle with the notion of object names, we have to return to the studies of the socio-perceptual skills of infants that were reviewed in Chapter 3. As we saw there, during the first year of life, the child develops several abilities that are important for lexical development. These are abilities that allow the child and adult to establish joint reference and they involve the development of joint visual attention—learning to look where someone else is looking—and the production and comprehension of pointing. These skills are, in turn, possible because young infants have a surprisingly sophisticated knowledge of objects and their properties (for recent reviews, see Butterworth, 1989; P. Harris, 1989; Slater, 1989; Willatts, 1989).

As Dunlea points out, establishing joint attention to objects out there in the world is very difficult for the blind child. Because of this, it seems very likely that initially the blind child's experience of hearing adults use words will be significantly different from that of a sighted child and this will have important implications for lexical development. For, as we saw in Chapter 7, even when sighted children first begin to use words, at least some of their uses involve contextually flexible object reference. This implies that, at the outset of production, sighted children are already able to pick out and refer to objects in their environment (as studies of the development of pointing suggest). Such an ability does not appear to be present in the blind child at the same stage and so we can see that, when blind children first start to produce words, they do so without the same degree of socio-perceptual competence. And it is this difference which leads to the very conservative and context-bound nature of much of the blind child's early lexicon and to its relatively linear development.

Why Children are Smarter than Chimpanzees

At this point it is tempting to begin another book because so many issues arise from an attempt to understand all the various social and perceptual factors that are important in the development of the early lexicon (see Zukow, 1990, for a recent discussion). However, I want to end on a slightly different note because the findings of Dunlea's study reminded me of another study of the early lexicon that was referred to earlier (see Chapter 1). This is the Savage-Rumbaugh et al. (1986) study of the pygmy chimpanzee, Kanzi.

What struck me was that, in two important respects, the early lexicon of the blind child and the pygmy chimpanzee are rather similar. First, both studies report that lexical development proceeded at a steady rate and there was no characteristic spurt in the rate of acquisition. Secondly, both the blind children and the pygmy chimpanzee tended to use a word in a way that was very close to the specific context in which that word had actually been encountered. There is an important difference though. Dunlea reports that, for the first 100 words, the blind children's use was rigid in that they were unwilling to extend their initial use of words either beyond the scope of their own action or to unfamiliar objects. However, there is no reason to suppose that this tendency persisted. Older blind children and adults find no difficulty in using new words in a contextually flexible fashion or in grasping the notion of reference. For the chimpanzee, however, there is a different pattern. Savage-

Rumbaugh reports that both Kanzi and Mulika (Kanzi's younger half-sister) often began to use symbols within usage routines. She notes that: "In fact, most new symbols seem to appear in such routines for some time before they reach a stage of referential functioning" (Savage-Rumbaugh et al., 1986, p.220). In other words, Kanzi and Mulika continued to acquire new symbols in an initially context-bound way and did not move to the point where new words were used in a contextually flexible and referential fashion right from the outset.

What is interesting about considering these two studies together is that they highlight the importance of being able to establish reference. The difference between them in this regard is that, for the blind child, learning to refer takes longer than for a sighted child because reference is normally established through visually mediated processes. However, for the chimpanzee, the notion of reference never appears to fully develop.

One reason for thinking that chimpanzees are not capable of reference in the same sense as human beings is that they do not point. As we saw in Chapter 3, they can indicate by stretching out an arm but the very specific pointing gesture, with index finger extended, is uniquely human. If the ability to point (and to check that your point has been perceived) is an indication that a child can pick out an object in the world and draw the attention of another person to it, then this is an ability that the chimpanzee does not appear to possess. The implications of this are that the chimpanzee will remain in the first phase of lexical development. As we saw in Chapter 6, the initial phase can be seen as one in which the child discovers what words are and what functions they perform. An essential aspect of this is the realisation that words can be used to refer. Such a realisation appears to be beyond the scope of the chimpanzee, although this is not to deny that the pygmy chimp can learn that some things have names.

We can see, then, that explaining the role of language experience in early language development is no simple task. Certain features of what the child hears are undoubtedly important, notably consistent adult use of particular words in familiar non-verbal contexts. And I have argued that, in the absence of opportunities to observe consistent relationships, early lexical development will be more problematic for the child. However, it is also clear that the child interprets language experience in the light of certain kinds of non-linguistic information about the world and the development of the early lexicon is the result of a complex interplay between social, perceptual and linguistic experience. What we need for the future is accounts that bring together all these various factors.

References

Atkinson, M. (1987). Mechanisms for language acquisition: Learning, parameter-setting and triggering. *First Language, 7,* 3–30.

Barnes, S., Gutfreund, M., Satterly, D. & Wells, G. (1983). Characteristics of adult speech which predict children's language development. *Journal of Child Language, 10,* 65–84.

Barrett, M. (1986). Early semantic representations and early semantic development. In S.A. Kuczaj & M. Barrett (Eds.), *The development of word meaning.* New York: Springer-Verlag.

Barrett, M. (1989). Early language development. In A. Slater & G. Bremner (Eds.), *Infant development.* Hove: Lawrence Erlbaum Associates Ltd.

Barrett, M., Harris, M. & Chasin, J. (1991). Early lexical development and maternal speech: A comparison of children's initial and subsequent uses. *Journal of Child Language, 18,* 21–40.

Barrett, M., Harris, M., Jones, D. & Brookes, S. (1986). Linguistic input and early context bound word use. In *Proceedings of the Child Language Seminar.* Department of Psychology, University of Durham.

Bates, E., Benigni, L., Bretherton, I., Camaioni, L. & Volterra, V. (1979). *The emergence of symbols: Cognition and communication in infancy.* New York: Academic Press.

Bates, E., Bretherton, I. & Snyder, L. (1988). *From first words to grammar: Individual differences and dissociable mechanisms.* Cambridge: Cambridge University Press.

Bauer, P.J. & Mandler, J.M. (1987). *What's in a name? Novel labels and taxonomic classification by 16- and 20-month olds.* Paper presented to the Biennial Meeting of the Society for Research in Child Development, Baltimore, MD.

Benedict, H. (1976). *Language comprehension in the 10–16-month-old infants.* Unpublished PhD Thesis, Yale University.

Bigelow, A. (1983). Development of the use of sound in the search behavior of infants. *Developmental Psychology, 19,* 317–321.

Botha, R.P. (1989). *Challenging Chomsky: The generative garden game.* Oxford: Blackwell.

Bower, T.G. (1974). *A primer of infant development.* San Francisco: Freeman.

Bowerman, M. (1976). Semantic factors in the acquisition of rules for word use and sentence construction. In D.M. Morehead & A.E. Morehead (Eds.), *Normal and deficient child language.* Baltimore, MD: University Park Press.

Brown, R.W. (1973). *A first language: The early stages.* Cambridge, MA: Harvard University Press.

Bruner, J.S. (1975a). The ontogenesis of speech acts. *Journal of Child Language, 2,* 1–19.

Bruner, J.S. (1975b). From communication to language—a psychological perspective. *Cognition, 3,* 255–287.

Bruner, J.S. (1983a). *Child's talk.* Cambridge: Cambridge University Press.

Bruner, J.S. (1983b). The acquisition of pragmatic commitments. In R.M. Golinkoff (Ed.), *The transition from prelinguistic to linguistic communication.* Hillsdale, NJ: Lawrence Erlbaum Associates Inc.

Bruner, J.S., Olver, R.R. & Greenfield, P.M. (1966). *Studies in cognitive growth.* New York: Wiley.

Budwig, N. & Wiley, A. (1991, April). *The contribution of caregivers' input to children's talk about agency and pragmatic control.* Paper presented to the 1991 Child Language Seminar. University of Manchester, Manchester.

Butterworth, G.E. (1989). Events and encounters in infant perception. In A. Slater & G. Bremner (Eds.), *Infant development.* Hove: Lawrence Erlbaum Associates Ltd.

Butterworth, G.E. (1991). The ontogeny and phylogeny of joint visual attention. In A. Whiten (Ed.), *Natural theories of mind.* Oxford: Blackwell.

Butterworth, G.E. & Franco, F. (1990). Motor development: Communication and cognition. In L. Kalverboer, B. Hopkins & R.H. Gueze (Eds.), *A longitudinal approach to the study of motor development in early and later childhood.* Cambridge: Cambridge University Press.

Butterworth, G.E. & Grover, L. (1989). Joint visual attention, manual pointing, and preverbal communication in human infancy. In M. Jeannerod (Ed.), *Attention and performance XIII.* Hove: Lawrence Erlbaum Associates Ltd.

Butterworth, G.E. & Jarrett, N. (1991). What minds have in common is space: Spatial mechanisms serving joint attention in infancy. *British Journal of Developmental Psychology, 9,* 55–72.

Carey, S. & Bartlett, E. (1978). Acquiring a new word. *Papers and Reports on Child Language Development, 15,* 17–29.

Caselli, M.C. (1983). Communication to language: Deaf children's and hearing children's development compared. *Sign Language Studies, 39,* 113–114.

Caselli, M.C. (1987). Language acquisition in Italian deaf children. In J.G. Kyle (Ed.), *Sign and school: Using sign in deaf children's development.* Clevedon, PA: Multi-Lingual Matters.

Chomsky, N. (1959). Review of *Verbal Behavior* by B.F. Skinner. *Language, 35,* 26–58.

Chomsky, N. (1965). *Aspects of the theory of syntax.* Cambridge, MA: MIT Press.
Chomsky, N. (1979). Interview with Brian McGee. In B. McGee (Ed.), *Men of ideas.* London: BBC Publications.
Chomsky, N. (1980). Rules and representations. *The Behavioural and Brain Sciences, 3,* 1–15; 42–61.
Chomsky, N. (1986). *Knowledge of language: Its nature, origins and use.* New York: Praeger.
Collis, G.M. (1977). Visual coorientation and maternal speech. In H.R. Schaffer (Ed.), *Studies of mother–infant interaction.* London: Academic Press.
Collis, G.M. (1985). On the origins of turn-taking: Alternation and meaning. In M.D. Barrett (Ed.), *Children's single-word speech.* Chichester: Wiley.
Collis, G.M. & Schaffer, H.R. (1975). Synchronization of visual attention in mother–infant pairs. *Journal of Child Psychology and Child Psychiatry, 16,* 315–320.
Cromer, R.F. (1979). The strengths of the weak form of the cognition hypothesis for language acquisition. In V. Lee (Ed.), *Language development.* London: Croom Helm.
Cross, T.G. (1977). Mothers' speech adjustment: The contributions of selected child listener variables. In C.E. Snow & C.A. Ferguson (Eds.), *Talking to children: Language input and interaction.* Cambridge: Cambridge University Press.
Cross, T.G. (1978). Mothers' speech and its association with rate of linguistic development in young children. In N. Waterson & C.E. Snow (Eds.), *The development of communication.* Chichester: Wiley.
Cross, T.G., Johnson-Morris, J.E. & Nienhuys, T.G. (1980). Linguistic feedback and maternal speech: Comparisons of mothers addressing hearing and hearing-impaired children. *First Language, 1,* 163–189.
Cuckle, P. & Karmiloff-Smith, A. (1988). Review of M. Harris & M. Coltheart, "Language Processing in Children and Adults". *Mind and Language, 3,* 152–157.
Curtiss, S. (1977). *Genie: A psycholinguistic study of a modern-day "wild child".* New York: Academic Press.
Dawkins, R. (1986). *The blind watchmaker.* Harlow: Longman.
Donaldson, M. & Wales, R. (1970). On the acquisition of some relational terms. In J.R. Hayes (Ed.), *Cognition and the development of language.* New York: Wiley.
Dore, J. (1978). Conditions for the acquisition of speech acts. In I. Markova (Ed.), *The social context of language.* New York: Wiley.
Dore, J. (1985). Holophrases revisited: Their "logical" development from dialogue. In M.D. Barrett (Ed.), *Children's single-word speech.* Chichester: Wiley.
Dromi, E. (1986). The one-word period as a stage in language development: Quantitative and qualitative accounts. In J. Levin (Ed.), *Stage and structure.* Norwood, NJ: Ablex.
Dromi, E. (1987). *Early lexical development.* Cambridge: Cambridge University Press.
Dunlea, A. (1989). *Vision and the emergence of meaning.* Cambridge: Cambridge University Press.
Durrell, M. (1988). Some problems of contrastive lexical semantics. In W. Hullen & R. Schulze (Eds.), *Understanding the lexicon: Meaning, sense and world knowledge in lexical semantics.* Tubingen: Verlag.
Ellis, R. & Wells, G. (1980). Enabling factors in adult–child discourse. *First Language, 1,* 46–62.

Filmore, C. (1968). The case for case. In E. Bach & T. Harms (Eds.), *Universals in linguistic theory*. New York: Holt, Rinehart and Winston.

Fodor, J. (1983). *The modularity of mind*. Cambridge, MA: MIT Press.

Folven, R.J., Bonvillian, J.D. & Orlansky, M.D. (1984/5). Communicative gestures and early sign language acquisition. *First Language, 5*, 89–100.

Fouts, R.S. (1972). Use of guidance in teaching sign language to chimpanzees. *Journal of Comparative and Physiological Psychology, 80*, 515–522.

Fraiberg, S. (1977). *Insights from the blind child*. New York: Basic Books.

Fraiberg, S., Siegal, B. & Gibson, R. (1966). The role of sound in the search behavior of a blind infant. *Psychoanalytic Study of the Child, 21*, 327–357.

Freedman, D.G. (1964). Smiling in blind infants and the issues of innate versus acquired. *Journal of Psychology and Psychiatry and Allied Disciplines, 5*, 171–184.

Furrow, D. & Nelson, K. (1984). Environmental correlates of individual differences in language acquisition. *Journal of Child Language, 11*, 523–534.

Furrow, D., Nelson, K. & Benedict, H. (1979). Mothers' speech to children and syntactic development: Some simple relationships. *Journal of Child Language, 6*, 423–442.

Gardner, B.T. & Gardner, R.A. (1971). Two-way communication with an infant chimpanzee. In A.M. Schrier & F. Stollnitz (Eds.), *Behavior of nonhuman primates*, Vol.4. New York: Academic Press.

Gardner, R.A. & Gardner, B.T. (1974). A vocabulary test for chimpanzees. *Journal of Comparative Psychology, 98*, 381–404.

Gleitman, L.R., Newport, E.L. & Gleitman, H. (1984). The current status of the motherese hypothesis. *Journal of Child Language, 11*, 43–79.

Gregory, S. & Barlow, S. (1988). Interactions between deaf babies and their deaf and hearing mothers. In B. Woll (Ed.), *Language development and sign language*. Bristol: International Sign Linguistics Association.

Gunzi, S. (unpublished). *Early language comprehension and production*.

Halliday, M.A.K. (1975). *Learning how to mean: Explorations in the development of language*. London: Arnold.

Harris, M. (1987). Review of B. Landau & L.R. Gleitman, "Language and experience: Evidence from the blind child". *Mind and Language, 2*, 350–353.

Harris, M. (1992). The relationship of maternal speech to children's first words. In D. Messer & G. Turner (Eds.), *Critical influences on language acquisition and development*. London: Macmillan.

Harris, M. & Barrett, M. (1989). Children's first words and their relation to maternal speech. In *Proceedings of the 1989 Child Language Seminar*. Department of Psychology, Hatfield Polytechnic.

Harris, M., Barrett, M., Jones, D. & Brookes, S. (1988). Linguistic input and early word meaning. *Journal of Child Language, 15*, 77–94.

Harris, M., Clibbens, J., Chasin, J. & Tibbitts, R. (1989). The social context of early sign language development. *First Language, 9*, 81–97.

Harris, M. & Coltheart, M. (1986). *Language processing in children and adults*. London: Routledge.

Harris, M. & Davies, M. (1987). Learning and triggering in child language: A reply to Atkinson. *First Language, 7*, 31–39.

Harris, M., Jones, D. & Grant, J. (1983). The nonverbal context of mothers' speech to children. *First Language, 4*, 21–30.

Harris, M., Jones, D. & Grant, J. (1984/5). The social-interactional context of maternal speech to children: An explanation for the event-bound nature of early word use? *First Language, 5,* 89–100.

Harris, M., Jones, D., Brookes, S. & Grant, J. (1986). Relations between the non-verbal context of maternal speech and rate of language development. *British Journal of Developmental Psychology, 4,* 261–268.

Harris, M., Yeeles, C. & Oakley, Y. (1991, April). *The development of comprehension in the first year of life.* Paper presented to the 1991 Child Language Seminar. University of Manchester, Manchester.

Harris, M., Yeeles, C., Chasin, J., & Oakley, Y. (in prep.). *Symmetries and asymmetries in early lexical comprehension and production.*

Harris, P. (1989). Object permanence in infancy. In A. Slater & G. Bremner (Eds.), *Infant development.* Hove: Lawrence Erlbaum Associates Ltd.

Hoff-Ginsberg, E. (1990, July). *Social class, maternal speech and child language development.* Paper presented to the Fifth International Congress for the Study of Child Language. Budapest, Hungary.

Hudson, J. & Nelson, K. (1984). Play with language: Overextensions as analogies. *Journal of Child Language, 11,* 337–346.

Huttenlocher, J. & Smiley, P. (1987). Early word meanings: The case of object names. *Cognitive Psychology, 19,* 63–89.

Kampfe, C.M. & Turecheck, A.G. (1987). Reading achievement of prelingually deaf students and its relationship to parental method of communication. *American Annals of the Deaf, 132,* 11–15.

Karmiloff-Smith, A. (1979). *A functional approach to child language: A study of determiners and reference.* Cambridge: Cambridge University Press.

Kyle, J. & Allsop, J. (1982). *Deaf people and the community.* Final Report to the Nuffield Foundation.

Landau, B. & Gleitman, L.R. (1985). *Language and experience: Evidence from the blind child.* Cambridge, MA: Harvard University Press.

Leung, E.H.L. & Rheingold, H. (1981). Development of pointing as a social gesture. *Developmental Psychology, 17,* 215–220.

Lewis, C. & Gregory, S. (1987). Parents' talk to their infants. *First Language, 7,* 201–216.

Lewis, V. (1987). *Development and handicap.* Oxford: Blackwell.

Lucariello, J. (1987). Concept formation and its relation to word learning and use in the second year. *Journal of Child Language, 14,* 309–332.

Markman, E.M. & Hutchinson, J.E. (1984). Children's sensitivity to constraints on word meaning: Taxonomic versus thematic relations. *Cognitive Psychology, 16,* 1–27.

Masur, E.F. (1982). Mothers' responses to infants' object-related gestures: Influences on lexical development. *Journal of Child Language, 9,* 23–30.

McShane, J. (1979). The development of naming. *Linguistics, 13,* 155–161.

Messer, D.J. (1978). The integration of mothers' referential speech with joint play. *Child Development, 49,* 781–787.

Messer, D.J. (1980). The episodic structure of maternal speech to young children. *Journal of Child Language, 7,* 29–40.

Messer, D.J. (1983). The redundancy between adult speech and nonverbal interaction: A contribution to acquisition? In R.M. Golinkoff (Ed.), *The transition from prelinguistic to linguistic communication.* Hillsdale, NJ: Lawrence Erlbaum Associates Inc.

Mills, A. (1987). The language of the blind child: Normal or abnormal? In *Proceedings of the 1987 Child Language Seminar.* University of Durham, Durham.

Nelson, K. (1973). *Structure and strategy in learning to talk.* Monographs of the Society for Research in Child Development No. 38.

Nelson, K. (1987). What's in a name? Reply to Seidenberg and Petitto. *Journal of Experimental Psychology: General, 116,* 293–296.

Nelson, K. (1983). The derivation of concepts and categories from event representations. In E. Scholnick (Ed.), *New trends in conceptual representations.* Hillsdale, NJ: Lawrence Erlbaum Associates Inc.

Nelson, K. (1988). Constraints on word learning? *Cognitive Development, 3,* 221–246.

Nelson, K.E. & Bonvillian, J.D. (1978). Early language development: Conceptual growth and related processes between 2 and 4 1/2 years. In K.E. Nelson (Ed.), *Children's language,* Vol. 1. New York: Gardner.

Nelson, K. & Lucariello, J. (1985). The development of meaning in first words. In M. Barrett (Ed.), *Children's single-word speech.* Chichester: Wiley.

Newport, E.L., Gleitman, H. & Gleitman, L.R. (1977). Mother I'd rather do it myself: Some effects and non-effects of maternal speech style. In C. Snow & C.A. Ferguson (Eds.), *Talking to children: Language input and acquisition.* Cambridge: Cambridge University Press.

Ninio, A. (1992). Is early speech situational? An examination of some current theories about the relation of early utterances to context. In D. Messer & G. Turner (Eds.), *Critical influences on language acquisition and development.* London: Macmillan.

Ochs, E. & Schieffelin, B. (1984). Language acquisition and socialisation: Three developmental stories and their implications. In R. Shweder & R. LeVine (Eds.), *Culture and its acquisition.* Cambridge: Cambridge University Press.

Petitto, L.A. (1988). Knowledge of language in signed and spoken language acquisition. In B. Woll (Ed.), *Language development and sign language.* Bristol: International Sign Linguistics Association.

Petitto, L.A. & Seidenberg, M.S. (1979). On the evidence for linguistic abilities in signing apes. *Brain and Language, 8,* 162–183.

Phillips, J. (1973). Syntax and vocabulary of mothers' speech to young children: Age and sex comparisons. *Child Development, 44,* 182–185.

Premack, D. (1986). *Gavagai! or the future history of the animal language controversy.* Cambridge, MA: MIT Press.

Pye, C. (1986). Quiché Mayan speech to children. *Journal of Child Language, 13,* 85–100.

Quigley, S.P. & Paul, P.V. (1984). *Language and deafness.* London: Croom Helm.

Quine, W.V. (1960). *Word and object.* Cambridge, MA: MIT Press.

Reddy, V. (1990, September). *Humorous communication in the first year of life.* Paper presented to the 4th European Developmental Psychology Conference. University of Stirling, Glasgow.

Reddy, V. (1991). Playing with others' expectations: Teasing and mucking about in the first year. In A. Whiten (Ed.), *Natural theories of mind.* Oxford: Blackwell.

Rescorla, L.A. (1980). Overextension in early language development. *Journal of Child Language, 7,* 321–335.

Richards, B. (1990). *Language development and individual differences.* Cambridge: Cambridge University Press.

Savage-Rumbaugh, E.S. (1986). *Ape language: From conditioned responses to symbols.* New York: Columbia University Press.

Savage-Rumbaugh, E.S. (1987). Communication, symbolic communication and language: Reply to Seidenberg and Petitto. *Journal of Experimental Psychology: General, 116,* 288–292.

Savage-Rumbaugh, E.S., McDonald, K., Sevcik, R.A., Hopkins, W.D. & Rupert, E. (1986). Spontaneous symbol acquisition and communicative use by pygmy chimpanzees (*Pan paniscus*). *Journal of Experimental Psychology: General, 115,* 211–235.

Savage-Rumbaugh, E.S. & Wilkerson, B.J. (1978). Socio-sexual behavior in *Pan paniscus* and *Pan troglodytes*: A comparative study. *Journal of Human Evolution, 7,* 327–344.

Schaffer, H.R. (1975). Social development in infancy. In R. Lewin (Ed.), *Child alive.* London: Temple Smith.

Schaffer, H.R. (1984). *The child's entry into the social world.* London: Academic Press.

Schaffer, H.R. (1989a). Early social development. In A. Slater & G. Bremner (Eds.), *Infant development.* Hove: Lawrence Erlbaum Associates Ltd.

Schaffer, H.R. (1989b). Language in context. In S. von Tetzchner, L.S. Siegel & L. Smith (Eds.) *The social and cognitive aspects of early language development.* London: Springer-Verlag.

Schaffer, H.R., Collis, G.M. & Parsons, G. (1977). Vocal interchange and visual regard in verbal and preverbal children. In H.R. Schaffer (Ed.), *Studies in mother–infant interaction.* London: Academic Press.

Schieffelin, B. & Ochs, E. (1983). A cultural perspective on the transition from prelinguistic to linguistic communication. In R.M. Golinkoff (Ed.), *The transition from prelinguistic to linguistic communication.* Hillsdale, NJ: Lawrence Erlbaum Associates Inc.

Schwartz, T.G. & Terrell, B.Y. (1983). The role of input frequency in lexical acquisition. *Journal of Child Language, 10,* 57–64.

Seidenberg, M.S. & Petitto, L.A. (1979). Signing behaviour in apes: A critical review. *Cognition, 7,* 177–215.

Seidenberg, M.S. & Petitto, L.A. (1987). Communication, symbolic communication and language: Comment on Savage-Rumbaugh et al. *Journal of Experimental Psychology: General, 116,* 279–287.

Skinner, B.S. (1957). *Verbal behavior.* New York: Appleton-Century-Crofts.

Slater, A. (1989). Visual memory and perception in early infancy. In A. Slater & G. Bremner (Eds.), *Infant development.* Hove: Lawrence Erlbaum Associates Ltd.

Snow, C.E. (1972). Mothers' speech to children learning language. *Child Development, 43,* 549–565.

Snow, C.E. (1977). Mothers' speech research: From input to interaction. In C.E. Snow & C.A. Ferguson (Eds.), *Talking to children: Language input and acquisition.* Cambridge: Cambridge University Press.

Stemmer, N. (1989). Empiricist versus prototype theories of language acquisition. *Mind and Language, 4,* 201–221.

Swisher, M.V. (1986). *Conversational interaction between deaf children and their hearing mothers: The role of visual attention.* Paper presented to the Conference on Theoretical Issues in Sign Language Research. Rochester, NY.

Swisher, M.V. & Christie, K. (1988). Communications using a sign code for English: Interaction between deaf mothers and their infants. In B. Woll (Ed.), *Language development and sign language*. Bristol: International Sign Linguistics Association.

Terrace, H.S. (1979). *Nim*. New York: Alfred A. Knopf.

Terrace, H.S. (1985). In the beginning was the "name". *American Psychologist, 40*, 1011–1028.

Todo, S., Fogel, A. & Kawai, M. (1990). Maternal speech to three-month-old infants in the United States and Japan. *Journal of Child Language, 17*, 279–294.

Tomasello, M. & Farrar, M.J. (1986). Joint attention and early language. *Child Development, 57*, 1454–1463.

Trevarthen, C. (1975). Early attempts at speech. In R. Lewin (Ed.), *Child alive*. London: Temple Smith.

Volterra, V. (1981). Gestures, signs and words at two years: When does communication become language? *Sign Language Studies, 33*, 351–362.

Volterra, V. & Caselli, M. C. (1985). From gestures and vocalisations to signs and words. In W. Stokoe & V. Volterra (Eds.), *SLR '83*. Silver Spring, MD: Linstok Press.

Walker, S.F. (1984). *Learning theory and behaviour modification*. London: Routledge.

Walker, S.F. (1987). Review of "Gavagai! or the Future History of the Animal Language Controversy" by D. Premack. *Mind and Language, 2*, 326–332.

Wells, G. (1981). *Learning through interaction: The study of language development*. Cambridge: Cambridge University Press.

Wexler, K. & Culicover, P. (1980). *Formal principles of language acquisition*. Cambridge, MA: MIT Press.

Willatts, P. (1989). Development of problem-solving in infancy. In A. Slater & G. Bremner (Eds.), *Infant development*. Hove: Lawrence Erlbaum Associates Ltd.

Woll, B. & Kyle, J. (1989). Communication and language development in children of deaf parents. In S. von Tetzchner, L.S. Siegel & L. Smith (Eds.), *The social and cognitive aspects of normal and atypical language development*. New York: Springer-Verlag.

Wood, D., Wood, H., Griffiths, A. & Howarth, I. (1986). *Teaching and talking with deaf children*. Chichester: Wiley.

Woollett, A. (1986). The influence of older siblings on the language environment of young children. *British Journal of Developmental Psychology, 4*, 235–245.

Yoder, P.Y. & Kaiser, A.P. (1989). Alternative explanations for the relationship between maternal verbal interactional style and child language development. *Journal of Child Language, 16*, 141–160.

Zukow, P.G. (1990). Socio-perceptual bases for the emergence of language: An alternative to innatist approaches. *Developmental Psychobiology, 23*, 705–726.

Zukow, P.G., Reilly, J. & Greenfield, P.M. (1982). Making the absent present: Facilitating the transition from sensorimotor to linguistic communication. In K.E. Nelson (Ed.), *Children's language*, Vol. 3. Hillsdale, NJ: Lawrence Erlbaum Associates Inc.

Author Index

Subject Index

Other Titles in the Series
Essays in Developmental Psychology
Series Editors: Peter Bryant, George Butterworth, Harry McGurk

Social Interaction And The Development Of Language & Cognition

ALISON F. GARTON
(Health Department of Western Australia)

This book identifies important research areas where social interaction has been considered in relation to children's language development and children's cognitive development. By incorporating research from major areas in developmental psychology, a unique conceptual contribution is made by the author. Further, an integrative analysis of the various theoretical positions considered provides the basis for unification of the different perspectives.

The author sets the scene by describing theories of development that have had a major impact on research concerned with the influence of social interaction on linguistic and cognitive development. Subsequent chapters critically discuss and evaluate research on social interaction and language development and how social aspects of the interaction process assist language development. An argument is developed that permits the postulation of social mechanisms in interaction that mediate to facilitate both linguistic and cognitive growth during development from infancy to middle childhood.

This book differs from others in the field by integrating in a unique way a diverse range of contemporary developmental research. Traditional demarcation between areas of research studies is ignored in an attempt to reconcile both empirical evidence and theoretical perspectives. In addition, a synthesising position is developed, incorporating aspects of the research and theories presented throughout the book, which advocates the facilitary role of active social interaction in both language and cognitive development. Recent research extensions of social interaction as applied to the realm of academic learning are highlighted.

ISBN 0-86377-227-7 1991 176pp. $25.50 £14.95 hbk.

Please send USA & Canadian orders to: Lawrence Erlbaum Associates Inc., 365 Broadway, Hillsdale, New Jersey, NJ07642, USA. For UK & Rest of World, please send orders to: Lawrence Erlbaum Associates Ltd., Mail Order Department, 27 Church Road, Hove, East Sussex, BN3 2FA, England. Note, prices shown here are correct at time of going to press, but may change. Prices outside Europe may differ from those shown.

Essays in Developmental Psychology

Series Editors: Peter ___, ___, Harry McGurk

THE DEVELOPMENT OF YOUNG CHILDREN'S SOCIAL-COGNITIVE

Understan___ ___cial world
has becom___ ___he last 25
years rese___ ___mirror the
confluenc___ ___lopmental
psycholog___ ___emes and
findings ___ ___h, and to
present a r___ ___cognitive
skills. Bey___ ___s synopsis
articulates ___ ___rocessing,
Piagetian a___ ___tual basis
for underst___

Buildir___ ___ntal
psycholog___ ___ther the
advantages ___ ___e
considerab ___ ___archers
and Goffm___ ___d
around the ___ ___onal
contexts, th___

The fr___ ___ntal
social cog___
conversat___
developm___ ___en's
participat___ ___ for
the frame___

Please send ___ Inc., 365
Broadway, ___ please send
orders to: La___ ___urch Road,
Hove, East ___ ___t at time of
going to pre___ ___shown.